Dances & Customs
of the
Indians of the South West

Dances & Customs
of the
Indians of the South West

A Collection of Classic Works on the Apache,
Zuni, Moquis and Pueblo Native American
Indian Tribes

John G. Bourke

LEONAUR

Dances & Customs of the Indians of the South West
A Collection of Classic Works on the Apache, Zuni, Moquis and Pueblo
Native American Indian Tribes
by John G. Bourke

FIRST EDITION

Compiled from the titles
The Medicine-Men of the Apache
The Urine Dance of the Zuni Indians of New Mexico
Compilation of Notes and Memoranda Bearing Upon the Use of Human Ordure and
Human Urine in Rites of a Religious or Semi-Religious Character
The Snake-Dance of the Moquis
and
The Moquis of Arizona

Leonaur is an imprint of Oakpast Ltd

Copyright in this form © 2012 Oakpast Ltd

ISBN: 978-0-85706-795-1 (hardcover)
ISBN: 978-0-85706-796-8 (softcover)

http://www.leonaur.com

Publisher's Notes

Contents

Letter of Transmittal

Washington, D. C., February 27, 1891.
Sir: Herewith I have the honour to submit a paper upon the paraphernalia of the medicine-men of the Apache and other tribes.

Analogues have been pointed out, wherever possible, especially in the case of the *hoddentin* and the *izze-kloth*, which have never to my knowledge previously received treatment.

I have the honour to be, very respectfully, your obedient servant,

John G. Bourke, Captain,

Third Cavalry, U. S. Army.

Hon. J. W. Powell,
Director Bureau of Ethnology.

9 Eth——29

The Medicine–Men

The Caucasian population of the United States has been in intimate contact with the aborigines for a period of not less than two hundred and fifty years. In certain sections, as in Florida and New Mexico, this contact has been for a still greater period; but claiming no earlier date than the settlement of New England, it will be seen that the white race has been slow to learn or the red man has been skilful in withholding knowledge which, if imparted, would have lessened friction and done much to preserve and assimilate a race that, in spite of some serious defects of character, will for all time to come be looked upon as "the noble savage."

Recent deplorable occurrences, (as at time of first publication), in the country of the Dakotas have emphasized our ignorance and made clear to the minds of all thinking people that, notwithstanding the acceptance by the native tribes of many of the improvements in living introduced by civilization, the savage has remained a savage, and is still under the control of an influence antagonistic to the rapid absorption of new ideas and the adoption of new customs.

This influence is the "medicine-man."

Who, and what are the medicine-men (or medicine-women), of the American Indians? What powers do they possess in time of peace or war? How is this power obtained, how renewed, how exercised? What is the character of the remedies employed? Are they pharmaceutical, as we employ the term, or are they the superstitious efforts of empirics and charlatans, seeking to deceive and to misguide by pretended consultations with spiritual powers and by reliance upon mysterious and occult influences?

9

Such a discussion will be attempted in this paper, which will be restricted to a description of the personality of the medicine-men, the regalia worn, and the powers possessed and claimed. To go farther, and enter into a treatment of the religious ideas, the superstitions, omens, and prayers of these spiritual leaders, would be to open a road without end.

As the subject of the paraphernalia of the medicine-men has never, to my knowledge, been comprehensively treated by any writer, I venture to submit what I have learned during the twenty-two years of my acquaintance with our savage tribes, and the studies and conclusions to which my observations have led. While treating in the main of the medicine-men of the Apache, I do not intend to omit any point of importance noted among other tribes or peoples.

First, in regard to the organization of the medicine-men of the Apache, it should be premised that most of my observations were made while the tribe was still actively engaged in hostilities with the whites, and they cannot be regarded as, and are not claimed to be, conclusive upon all points. The Apache are not so surely divided into medicine lodges or secret societies as is the case with the Ojibwa, as shown by Dr. W. J. Hoffman; the Siouan tribes, as related by Mr. J. Owen Dorsey; the Zuñi, according to Mr. F. H. Gushing; the Tusayan, as shown by myself, and other tribes described by other authorities.

The Navajo, who are the full brothers of the Apache, seem to have well denned divisions among their medicine-men, as demonstrated by Dr. Washington Matthews, U. S. Army; and I myself have seen great medicine lodges, which must have contained at least a dozen Apache medicine-men, engaged in some of their incantations. I have also been taken to several of the sacred caves, in which solemn religious dances and other ceremonies were conducted under the same superintendence, but never have I witnessed among the Apache any rite of religious significance in which more than four or five, or at the most six, of the medicine-men took part.

The difficulty of making an accurate determination was increased by the nomadic character of the Apache, who would always prefer to live in small villages containing only a few brush shelters, and not needing the care of more than one or two of their " doctors." These people show an unusual secretiveness and taciturnity in all that relates to their inner selves, and, living as they do in a region filled with caves and secluded nooks, on cliffs, and in deep canyons, have not been compelled to celebrate their sacred offices in *"estufas,"* or *"pla-*

zas," open to the inspection of the profane, as has been the case with so many of the Pueblo tribes.

Diligent and persistent inquiry of medicine-men whose confidence I had succeeded in gaining, convinced me that any young man can become a "doctor" ("*diyi*" in the Apache language, which is translated "*sabio*" by the Mexican captives). It is necessary to convince his friends that he "has the gift," as one of my informants expressed it; that is, he must show that he is a dreamer of dreams, given to long fasts and vigils, able to interpret omens in a satisfactory manner, and do other things of that general nature to demonstrate the possession of an intense spirituality. Then he will begin to withdraw, at least temporarily, from the society of his fellows and devote himself to long absences, especially by night, in the "high places" which were interdicted to the Israelites.

Such sacred fanes, perched in dangerous and hidden retreats, can be, or until lately could be, found in many parts in our remote western territory. In my own experiences I have found them not only in the country of the Apache, but two-thirds of the way up the vertical face of the dizzy precipice of Tâaiyalana, close to Zuñi, where there is a shrine much resorted to by the young men who seek to divine the result of a contemplated enterprise by shooting arrows into a long cleft in the smooth surface of the sandstone; I have seen them in the Wolf Mountains, Montana; in the Big Horn range, Wyoming; on the lofty sides of Cloud Peak, and elsewhere. Maj. W. S. Stanton, Corps of Engineers, U. S. Army, ascended the Cloud Peak twice, and, reaching the summit on the second attempt, he found that beyond the position first attained and seeming then to be the limit of possible ascent, some wandering Indian had climbed and made his "medicine."

While it is regarded as a surer mode of learning how to be a medicine-man to seek the tuition of someone who has already gained power and influence as such, and pay him liberally in presents of all kinds for a course of instruction lasting a year or longer, I could learn of nothing to prohibit a man from assuming the role of a prophet or healer of the sick, if so disposed, beyond the dread of punishment for failure to cure or alleviate sickness or infirmity. Neither is there such a thing as settled dogma among these medicine-men. Each follows the dictates of his own inclinations, consulting such spirits and powers as are most amenable to his supplications and charms; but no two seem to rely upon identically the same influences. Even in the spirit dance, which is possibly the most solemn function in which the

Apache medicine-men can engage, the head-dresses and kilts adhered closely enough to the one pattern, but the symbolism employed by each medicine-man was entirely different from that adopted by his neighbours.

Schultze, Perrin du Lac, Adair, and others allude to " houses of mercy," the "right of asylum" in certain lodges and buildings, or even whole villages, to which if the pursued of the tribe or even an enemy could obtain admission his life was secure. Frank Gruard and others who have lived for years among the Sioux, the Cheyenne, and other tribes of the plains have assured me that the same right of asylum obtains among them for the fugitive who takes shelter in the medicine lodge or the council lodge, and almost parallel notions prevail among the Apache. I have heard that the first American who came into one of their villages, tired and hungry, was not molested in the slightest degree.

It is stated by Kelly[1] that all warriors who go through the sun dance of the Sioux rank thereafter as medicine-men. This statement seems to me to be overdrawn. Nothing of the kind was learned by me at the, sun dance of the Sioux which I noted in 1881, and in any event the remark would scarcely apply to the medicine-men of the Apache, who have nothing clearly identifiable with the sun dance, and who do not cut, gash, or in any manner mutilate themselves, as did the principal participants in the sun dance, or as was done in still earlier ages by the *galli* (the priests of Cybele) or the priests of Mexico.

Herodotus tells us that the priests of Egypt, or rather the doctors, who were at one time identified with them, were separated into classes; some cured the eyes, some the ears, others the head or the belly. Such a differentiation is to be observed among the Apache, Mohave, and other tribes; there are some doctors who enjoy great fame as the bringers of rain, some who claim special power over snakes, and some who profess to consult the spirits only, and do not treat the sick except when no other practitioner may be available.

Among the Mohave, the relatives of a dead man will consult one of these spirit-doctors and get him to interview the ghosts who respond to his call and learn from them whether the patient died from ignorance or neglect on the part of the doctor who had charge of the case. If the spirits assert that he did, then the culprit doctor must either flee for his life or throw the onus of the crime upon some witch. This differentiation is not carried so far that a medicine-man, no matter what

---

1. *My Captivity among the Sioux Indians* by Fanny Kelly (also published by Leonaur).

his class, would decline a large fee.

The right of sanctuary was conceded to all criminals who sought shelter in the *vanquech* or temple of Chinigchinich.[2]

The Oregon tribes have spirit doctors and medicine doctors.[3]

In all nations in the infancy of growth, social or mental, the power to coax from reluctant clouds the fructifying rain has been regarded with highest approval and will always be found confided to the most important hierophants or devolving upon some of the most prominent deities; almighty Jove was a deified rain-maker or cloud-compeller. Rain-makers flourished in Europe down to the time of Charlemagne, who prohibited these "*tempestiarii*" from plying their trade.

One of the first requests made of Vaca and his comrades by the people living in fixed habitations near the Rio Grande was "to tell the sky to rain," and also to pray for it.[4]

There does not seem to have been any inheritance of priestly functions among the Apache or any setting apart of a particular clan or family for the priestly duties.

Francis Parkman is quoted as describing a certain family among the Miami who were reserved for the sacred ritualistic cannibalism perpetrated by that tribe upon captives taken in war. Such families devoted more or less completely to sacred uses are to be noted among the Hebrews (in the line of Levi) and others; but they do not occur in the tribes of the Southwest.

One of the ceremonies connected with the initiation, as with every exercise of spiritual functions by the medicine-man, is the "*ta-a-chi*," or sweat-bath, in which, if he be physically able, the patient must participate.

The Apache do not, to my knowledge, indulge in any poisonous intoxicants during their medicine ceremonies; but in this they differ to a perceptible degree from other tribes of America. The "black drink" of the Creeks and the "*wisoccan*" of the Virginians maybe cited as cases in point; and the Walapai of Arizona, the near neighbours of the Apache, make use of the juice, or a decoction of the leaves, roots, and flowers of the *Datura stramonium* to induce frenzy and exhilaration. The laurel grows wild on all the mountain tops of Sonora and Arizona, and the Apache credit it with the power of setting men crazy, but they deny that they have ever made use of it in their medicine or

2. Robinson's *California*.
3. Ross, *Fur Hunters Desc. Soc.*
4. Davis. *Spanish Conq. of N. M.*

religion.

Picart speaks of the drink (*wisoccan*) which took away the brains of the young men undergoing initiation as medicine-men among the tribes of Virginia, but he does not say what this "*wisoccan*" was.

I have never seen tobacco juice drank by medicine-men or others, but I remember seeing Shunca-Luta (Sorrel Horse) a medicine-man of the Dakota, chewing and swallowing a piece of tobacco and then going into what seemed to be a trance, all the while emitting deep grunts or groans.

When he revived he insisted that those sounds had been made by a spirit which he kept down in his stomach. He also pretended to extract the quid of tobacco from underneath his ribs, and was full of petty tricks of legerdemain and other means of mystifying women and children.

All medicine-men claim the power of swallowing spear heads or arrows and fire, and there are at times many really wonderful things done by them which have the effect of strengthening their hold upon the people.

The medicine-men of the Ojibwa thrust arrows and similar instruments down their throats. They also allow themselves to be shot at with marked bullets. [5]

While I was among the Tusayan, in 1881, I learned of a young boy, quite a child, who was looked up to by the other Indians, and on special occasions made his appearance decked out in much native finery of beads and gewgaws, but the exact nature of his duties and supposed responsibilities could not be ascertained.

I shall have occasion to introduce a medicine-woman of the Apache, Tze-go-juni, or "Pretty-mouth," whose claims to pre-eminence among her people would seem to have had no better foundation than her escape from lightning stroke and from the bites of a mountain lion, which had seized her during the night and had not killed her.

I remember the case of an old Navajo medicine-man who was killed by lightning. The whole tribe participated in the singing, drumming, and dancing incident to so important an event, but no white men were allowed to be present. My information was derived from the dead man's young nephew, while I was among that tribe.

Among the Arawak of South America there are hereditary conjurers who profess to find out the enemy who by the agency of an evil

5. Tanner's *Narrative*.

14

spirit has killed the deceased. [6]

Picart says of the medicine-men of the tribes along Rio de la Plata: "*Pour être Prêtre ou Médecin parmi eux, il fant avoir jeûne longtems & souvent. Il fant avoir combatu plusieurs fois contre les bêtes Sauvages, principalement contre les Tigres, & tout au moins en avoir été mordu ou égratigné. Après cela on peut obtenir l'Ordre, de Prêtrise; car le Tigre est chez eux un animal presque divin.*" [7] (To be a priest or physician among them there must be fasting long and often. You need to have several fights against wild beasts, mainly against tigers, and at least to have been bitten or scratched. After that you can get the Order of Priesthood, for the tiger itself is an almost divine animal.)

The medicine-men of the Apache are not confined to one gens or clan, as among the Shawnee and Cherokee, according to Brinton,[8] neither do they believe, as the Cherokee do, according to the same authority, that the seventh son is a natural-born prophet with the gift of healing by touch, but upon this latter point I must be discreet, as I have never known an Apache seventh son.

The Cherokee still preserve the custom of consecrating a family of their tribe to the priesthood, as the family of Levi was consecrated among the Jews. [9]

Peter Martyr says of the Chiribchis of South America: "Out of the multitude of children they chuse some of 10 or 12 yeeres old, whom they know by conjecture to be naturally inclined to that service."[10]

The peculiarity of the Moxos was that they thought none designated for the office of medicine-man but such as had escaped from the claws of the South American tiger which, indeed, it is said they worshiped as a god.[11]

Contrary to what Spencer says, the chiefs of the, tribes of the Southwest, at least, are not *ipso facto* medicine-men; but among the Tonto Apache the brother of the head chief, Cha-ut-lip-un, was the great medicine-man, and generally the medicine-men are related closely to the prominent chiefs, which would seem to imply either a formal deputation of priestly functions from the chiefs to relatives, or what may be practically the same thing, the exercise of family influence to bring about a recognition of the necromantic powers of some

6. Spencer, *Desc. Sociology.*

7. Picart, *Cérémonies et Coutumes Religieuses,* vol. 6.

8. *Myths of the New World.*

9. Domeuech, *Deserts,* vol. 2.

10. Hakluyt, *Voyages,* vol. 5.

11. Brinton, *Myths of the New World.*

aspirant; but among the Apache there is no priest *caste*; the same man may be priest, warrior, etc.[12]

> The Darien Indians used the seeds of the *Datura sanguinea* to bring on in children prophetic delirium, in which they revealed hidden treasure. In Peru the priests who talked with the "*huaca*" or fetishes used to throw themselves into an ecstatic condition by a narcotic drink called "*tonca,*" made from the same plant.
>
> —Tylor. *Primitive Culture*. vol. 2.

The medicine-men of the Walapai, according to Charlie Spencer, who married one of their women and lived among them for years, were in the habit of casting bullets in moulds which contained a small piece of paper. They would allow these bullets to be fired at them, and of course the missile would split in two parts and do no injury. Again, they would roll a ball of sinew and attach one end to a small twig, which was inserted between the teeth. They would then swallow the ball of sinew, excepting the end thus attached to the teeth, and after the heat and moisture of the stomach had softened and expanded the sinew they would begin to draw it out yard after yard, saying to the frightened squaws that they had no need of intestines and were going to pull them all out.

Others among the Apache have claimed the power to shoot off guns without touching the triggers or going near the weapons; to be able to kill or otherwise harm their enemies at a distance of 100 miles. In nearly every boast made there is some sort of a saving clause, to the effect that no witchcraft must be made or the spell will not work, no women should be near in a delicate state from any cause, etc.

Mickey Free has assured me that he has seen an Apache medicine-man light a pipe without doing anything but hold his hands up toward the sun. This story is credible enough if we could aver that the medicine-man was supplied, as I suspect he was, with a burning glass.

That the medicine-man has the faculty of transforming himself into a coyote and other animals at pleasure and then resuming the human form is as implicitly believed in by the American Indians as it was by our own forefathers in Europe. The Apache look upon blacksmiths as being allied to the spirits and call them "*pesh-chidin*"—the witch, spirit, or ghost, of the iron. The priestly powers conceded to the blacksmith of Gretna Green need no allusion here.

---

12. Spencer, *Ecclesiastical Institutions*, cap. v.

Parkman[13] describes, from the Relations of Père Le Jeune, how the Algonkin medicine-man announced that he was going to kill a rival medicine-man who lived at Gaspé, 100 leagues distant.

Great as are the powers claimed by the medicine-men, it is admitted that baleful influences may be at work to counteract and nullify them. As has already been shown, among these are the efforts of witches, the presence of women who are sometimes supposed to be so "antimedicinal," if such a term may be applied, that the mere stepping over a warrior's gun will destroy its value.

There may be other medicine-men at work with countercharms, and there may be certain neglects on the part of the person applying for aid which will invalidate all that the medicine-man can do for him. For example, while the "*hoop-me-koff*" was raging among the Mohave the fathers of families afflicted with it were forbidden to touch coffee or salt, and were, directed to bathe themselves in the current of the Colorado. But the whooping cough ran its course in spite of all that the medicine-men could do to check its progress. When the Walapai were about to engage in a great hunt continence was enjoined upon the warriors for a certain period.

Besides all these accidental impairments of the vigour of the medicine-men, there seems to be a gradual decadence of their abilities which can be rejuvenated only by rubbing the back against a sacred stone projecting from the ground in the country of the Walapai, not many miles from the present town of Kingman, on the Atlantic and Pacific Railroad. Another stone of the same kind was formerly used for the same purpose by the medicine-men of the *pueblos* of Laguna and Acoma, as I have been informed by them. I am unable to state whether or not such recuperative properties were ever ascribed to the medicine stone at the Sioux agency near Standing Rock, S. Dak., or to the great stone around which the medicine-men of Tusayan marched in solemn procession in their snake dance, but I can say that in the face of the latter, each time that I saw it (at different dates between 1874 and 1881), there was a niche which was filled with votive offerings.

Regnard, a traveller in Lapland, makes the statement that when the shamans of that country began to lose their teeth they retired from practice. There is nothing of this kind to be noted among the Apache or other tribes of North America with which I am in any degree familiar. On the contrary, some of the most influential of those whom I have known have been old and decrepit men, with thin, gray hair

13. *Jesuits in North America.*

and teeth gone or loose in their heads. In a description given by Corbusier of a great "medicine" ceremony of the Apache Yuma at Camp Verde, it is stated that the principal officer was a "toothless, gray-haired man."[14]

Among many savage or barbarous peoples of the world albinos have been reserved for the priestly office. There are many well marked examples of albinism among the Pueblos of New Mexico and Arizona, especially among the Zuñi and Tusayan; but in no case did I learn that the individuals thus distinguished were accredited with power not ascribable to them under ordinary circumstances. Among the Cheyenne I saw one family, all of whose members had the crown lock white. They were not medicine-men, neither were any of the members of the single albino family among the Navajo in 1881.

Our native tribes do not exactly believe that the mildly insane are gifted with medical or spiritual powers; but they regard them with a feeling of superstitious awe, akin to reverence. I have personally known several cases of this kind, though not within late years, and am not able to say whether or not the education of the younger generation in our schools has as yet exercised an influence in eradicating this sentiment. Strange to say, I was unable to find any observance of lucky or unlucky days among the Apache. In this the Apache again stands above the Roman who would not marry in the month dedicated to the goddess Maia (May), because human sacrifice used to be offered in that month.

Herbert Spencer [15] says that the medicine-men of the Arawaks claimed the "*jus primae noctis.*" There is no such privilege claimed or conceded among the North American tribes, to my knowledge, and the Arawaks would seem to be alone among the natives of the whole continent in this respect.

To recover stolen or lost property, especially ponies, is one of the principal tasks imposed upon the medicine-men. They rely greatly upon the aid of pieces of crystal in effecting this I made a friend of an Apache medicine-man by presenting him with a large crystal of denticulated spar, much larger than the one of whose mystical properties he had just been boasting to me. I cannot say how this property of the crystal is manifested. Na-a-cha, the medicine-man alluded to, could give no explanation, except that by looking into it he could see everything he wanted to see.

---

14. *American Antiquarian.*
15. *Descriptive Sociology.*

The name of an American Indian is a sacred thing, not to be divulged by the owner himself without due consideration. One may ask a warrior of any tribe to give his name and the question will be met with either a point-blank refusal or the more diplomatic evasion that he cannot understand what is wanted of him. The moment a friend approaches, the warrior first interrogated will whisper what is wanted, and the friend can tell the name, receiving a reciprocation of the courtesy from the other. The giving of names to children is a solemn matter, and one in which the medicine-men should always be consulted. Among the Plains tribes the children were formerly named at the moment of piercing their ears, which should occur at the first sun dance after their birth, or rather as near their first year as possible. The wailing of the children at the sun dance as their ears were slit will always be to me a most distressing memory.

The warriors of the Plains tribes used to assume agnomens or battle names, and I have known some of them who had enjoyed as many as four or five; but the Apache name once conferred seems to remain through life, except in the case of the medicine-men, who, I have always suspected, change their names upon assuming their profession, much as a professor of learning in China is said to do.

The names of mothers-in-law are never mentioned and it would be highly improper to ask for them by name; neither are the names of the dead, at least not for a long period of time. But it often happens that the child will bear the name of its grandfather or some other relative who was a distinguished warrior.

All charms, idols, talismans, medicine hats, and other sacred regalia should be made, or at least blessed, by the medicine-men. They assume charge of all ceremonial feasts and dances—such as the nubile dance, which occurs when any maiden attains marriageable age, and war dances preceding battle.

Nearly all preparations for the warpath are under their control, and when on the trail of the enemy their power is almost supreme. Not a night passes but that the medicine-men get into the "*ta-a-chi*," or sweat bath, if such a thing be possible, and there remain for some minutes, singing and making "medicine" for the good of the party. After dark they sit around the fire and sing and talk with the spirits and predict the results of the campaign. I have alluded quite fully to these points in a previous work.

When a man is taken sick the medicine-men are in the zenith of their glory. One or two will assume charge of the case, and the clansmen and friends of the patient are called upon to supply the fire and help out in the chorus. On such occasions the Apache use no music except a drum or a rawhide. The drum is nearly always improvised from an iron camp kettle, partially filled with water and covered with a piece of cloth, well soaped and drawn as tight as possible. The drumstick does not terminate in a ball, as with us, but is curved into a circle, and the stroke is not perpendicular to the surface, but is often given from one side to the other.

The American Indian's theory of disease is the theory of the Chaldean, the Assyrian, the Hebrew, the Greek, the Roman—all bodily disorders and ailments are attributed to the maleficence of spirits who must be expelled or placated. Where there is only one person sick, the exercises consist of singing and drumming exclusively, but dancing is added in all cases when an epidemic is raging in the tribe. The medicine-men lead off in the singing, to which the assistants reply with a refrain which at times has appeared to me to be antiphonal. Then the chorus is swelled by the voices of the women and larger children and rises and falls with monotonous cadence.

Prayers are recited, several of which have been repeated to me and transcribed; but very frequently the words are ejaculatory and confined to such expressions as "*ngashe*" (go away), and again there is to be noted the same mumbling of incoherent phrases which has been the stock in trade of medicine-men in all ages and places. This use of gibberish was admitted by the medicine-men, who claimed that the words employed and known only to themselves (each individual seemed to have his own vocabulary) were mysteriously effective in dispelling sickness of any kind. Gibberish was believed to be more potent in magic than was language which the practitioner or his dupes could comprehend.

Adair denies that Indians on the warpath or elsewhere depend upon their "*augurs*" for instruction and guidance.[16] Gomara is authority for the statement that the natives of Hispaniola never made war without consulting their medicine-men—"*no sin respuesta de los ídolos ó sin la de los sacerdotes, que adevinan.*" [17]

The medicine men of Chicora (our present South Carolina) sprinkled the warriors with the juice of a certain herb as they were about to engage in battle.[18]

---

16. *American Indians.*
17 & 18. Gomara. *Hist, de las Indias.*

The North American Indians are nowhere idolaters.

—Catlin, *N. A. Indians* vol. 2.

The adoption or retention of obsolete phraseology as a hieratic language which has been noted among many nations of the highest comparative development is a manifestation of the same mental process.

Gibberish was so invariable an accompaniment of the sacred antics of the medicine-men of Mexico that Fray Diego Duran warns his readers that if they see any Indian dancing and singing, or saying unintelligible words they represent the Gods. "*ó diciendo algunas palabras que no son inteligibles, pues es de saber que aquellos representaban Dioses.*"

Henry Youle Hind says:

The Dakotahs have a common and a sacred language. The conjurer, the war prophet, and the dreamer employ a language in which words are borrowed from other Indian tongues and dialects: they make much use of descriptive expressions, and use words apart from the ordinary signification. The Ojibways abbreviate their sentences and employ many elliptical forms of expression, so much so that half-breeds, quite familiar with the colloquial language, fail to comprehend a medicine-man when in the full flow of excited oratory.

"Blood may be stanched by the words *sicycuma, cucuma, neuma, cuma, uma, ma, a.*"—*Cockayno*, Leechdoms. vol. 1. There are numbers of these gibberish *formulae* given, but one is sufficient.

It must be conceded that the monotonous intonation of the medicine-men is not without good results, especially in such ailments as can be benefited by the sleep which such singing induces. On the same principle that petulant babies are lulled to slumber by the crooning of their nurses, the sick will frequently be composed to a sound and beneficial slumber, from which they awake refreshed and ameliorated. I can recall, among many other cases, those of Chaundezi ("Long Ear," or "Mule") and Chemihuevi-Sal, both chiefs of the Apache, who recovered under the treatment of their own medicine-men after our surgeons had abandoned the case. This recovery could be attributed only to the sedative effects of the chanting.

Adair, who was gifted with an excellent imagination, alludes to the possession of an "ark" by the medicine-men of the Creeks and other tribes of the Mississippi country, among whom he lived for so many years as a trader. The Apache have no such things; but I did see a sacred bundle or package, which I was allowed to feel, but not to open, and which I learned contained some of the lightning-riven twigs upon which they place such dependence. This was carried by a young medicine-man, scarcely out of his teens, during Gen. Crook's expedition into the Sierra Madre,[19] Mexico, in 1883, in pursuit of the hostile Chiricahua Apache. Maj. Frank North also told me that the Pawnee had a sacred package which contained, among other objects of veneration, the skin of an albino buffalo calf.

There are allusions by several authorities to the necessity of confession by the patient before the efforts of the medicine-men can prove efficacious.[20]

This confession, granting that it really existed, could well be compared to the warpath secret, which imposed upon all the warriors engaged the duty of making a clean breast of all delinquencies and secured them immunity from punishment for the same, even if they had been offenses against some of the other warriors present.

The Sioux and others had a custom of "striking the post" in their dances, especially the sun dance, and there was then an obligation upon the striker to tell the truth. I was told that the medicine-men were wont to strike with a club the stalagmites in the sacred caves of the Apache, but what else they did I was not able to ascertain.

Under the title of "*hoddentin*" will be found the statement made by one of the Apache as to the means employed to secure the presence of a medicine-man at the bedside of the sick. I give it for what it is worth, merely stating that Kohl, in his *Kitchi-Gami*, if I remember correctly, refers to something of the same kind where the medicine-man is represented as being obliged to respond to every summons made unless he can catch the messenger within a given distance and kick him.

There is very little discrepancy of statement as to what would happen to a medicine-man in case of failure to cure; but many conflicting stories have been in circulation as to the number of patients he would be allowed to kill before incurring risk of punishment. My own conclusions are that there is no truth whatever in the numbers alleged, either three or seven, but that a medicine-man would be in

19. *On the Border With Crook* and *An Apache Campaign in the Sierra Madre* by the same author John G. Bourke also published by Leonaur.
20. When the Carriers are severely sick, they often think that they shall not recover, unless they divulge to a priest or magician, every crime which they may have committed, which has hitherto been kept secret." Harmon's *Journal*. The Carriers or *Ta-kully* are Tinneh.

danger, under certain circumstances, if he let only one patient die on his hands. These circumstances would be the verdict of the spirit doctors that he was culpably negligent or ignorant. He could evade death at the hands of the patient's kinsfolk only by flight or by demonstrating that a witch had been at the bottom of the mischief.

The, medicine-men of the Natchez were put to death when they failed to cure.

The Apache attach as much importance to the necessity of "laying the manes" of their dead as the Romans did. They have not localized the site of the future world as the Mohave have, but believe that the dead remain for a few days or nights in the neighbourhood of the place where they departed from this life, and that they try to communicate with their living friends through the voice of the owl. If a relative hears this sound by night, or, as often happens, he imagines that he has seen the ghost itself, he hurries to the nearest medicine-man, relates his story, and carries out to the smallest detail the prescription of feast, singing, dancing, and other means of keeping the spirit in good humour on the journey which it will now undertake to the "house of spirits," the *"chidin-bi-kungua."* Nearly all medicine-men claim the power of going there at will, and not a few who are not medicine-men claim the same faculty.

The medicine-men of the Apache are paid by each patient or by his friends at the time they are consulted. There is no such thing as a maintenance fund, no system of tithes, nor any other burden for their support, although I can recall having seen while among the Zuñi one of the medicine-men who was making cane holders for the tobacco to be smoked at a coming festival, and whose fields were attended and his herds guarded by the other members of the tribe.

Among other customs was that of those who came to be cured, giving their bow and arrows, shoes, and beads to the Indians who accompanied Vaca and his companions." (But we must remember that Vaca and his comrades travelled across the continent as medicine-men.)

The Asinai extended as far east as the present city of Natchitoches (Nacogdoches).

As a general rule, the medicine-men do not attend to their own families, neither do they assist in cases of childbirth unless specially needed. To both these rules there are exceptions innumerable. While I was at San Carlos Agency, Surgeon Davis was sent for to help in a case of *uterine inertia,* and I myself have been asked in the *pueblo* of Nambe,

New Mexico, to give advice in a case of puerperal fever.

The medicine-men are accused of administering poisons to their enemies. Among the Navajo I was told that they would put finely pounded glass in food.

MEDICINE-WOMEN.

There are medicine-women as well as medicine-men among the Apache, with two of whom I was personally acquainted. One named "Captain Jack" was well advanced in years and physically quite feeble, but bright in intellect and said to be well versed in the lore of her people. She was fond of instructing her grandchildren, whom she supported, in the prayers and invocations to the gods worshiped by her fathers, and I have several times listened carefully and unobserved to these recitations and determined that the prayers were the same as those which had already been given to myself as those of the tribe.

The other was named Tze-go-juni, a Chiricahua, and a woman with a most romantic history. She had passed five years in captivity among the Mexicans in Sonora and had learned to speak Spanish with facility. A mountain lion had severely mangled her in the shoulder and knee, and once she had been struck by lightning; so that whether by reason of superior attainments or by appeal to the superstitious reverence of her comrades, she wielded considerable influence. These medicine-women devote their attention principally to obstetrics, and have many peculiar stories to relate concerning pre-natal influences and matters of that sort. Tze-go-juni wore at her neck the stone amulet, shaped like a spear, which is figured in the illustrations of this paper. The material was the silex from the top of a mountain, taken from a ledge at the foot of a tree which had been struck by lightning.

The fact that siliceous rock will emit sparks when struck by another hard body appeals to the reasoning powers of the savage as a proof that the fire must have been originally deposited therein by the, bolt of lightning. A tiny piece of this arrow or lance was broken off and ground into the finest powder, and then administered in water to women during time of gestation. I have found the same kind of arrows in use among the women of Laguna and other *pueblos*. This matter will receive more extended treatment in my coming monograph on "Stone Worship."

Mendieta is authority for the statement that the Mexicans had both medicine-men and medicine-women. The former attended to the sick men and the latter to the sick women. Some of the medicine-

women seem to have made an illicit use of the knowledge they had acquired, in which case both the medicine-woman and the woman concerned were put to death.

Gomara asserts that they were to be found among the Indians of Chjcora (South Carolina). He calls them *"viejas"* (old women).

Berual Diaz, in 1568, speaks of having, on a certain occasion, at the summit of a high mountain, found:

> . . . . . an Indian woman, very fat, and having with her a dog of that species, which they breed in order to eat, and which do not bark. This Indian was a witch; she was in the act of sacrificing the dog, which is a signal of hostility.

> The office of medicine-man though generally usurped by males does not appertain to them exclusively, and at the time of our visit the one most extensively known was a black (or *meztizo*) woman, who had acquired the most unbounded influence by shrewdness, joined to a hideous personal appearance, and a certain mystery with which she was invested.

> Creeks have medicine-women, as well as medicine-men.

The medicine-men and women of the Dakota "can cause ghosts to appear on occasion."

Speaking of the Chippewa, Spencer says:

Women may practice soothsaying, but the higher religious functions are performed only by men.

The medicine-men of the Apache—do not assume to live upon food different from that used by the laity. There are such things as sacred feasts among the tribes of North America as, for example, the feast of stewed puppy at the sun dance of the Sioux—but in these all people, share.

In the mortuary ceremonies of the medicine-men there is a difference of degree, but not of kind. The Mohave, however, believe that the medicine-men go to a heaven of their own. They also believe vaguely in four different lives after this one.

Cabeza de Vaca says that the Floridians buried their ordinary dead, but burned their medicine-men, whose incinerated bones they preserved and drank in water. "After they [the medicine-men and women of the Dakota] have four times run their career in human shape they are annihilated." Schultze says that the medicine-men of the Sioux and the medicine-women also, after death "maybe transformed into wild beasts."

Surgeon Smart shows that among other offices entrusted to the medicine-men of the Apache was the reception of distinguished strangers. Long asserts that the medicine-men of the Otoe, Omaha, and others along the Missouri pretended to be able to converse with the *fetus in utero* and predict the sex. Nothing of that kind has ever come under my notice. Adair says that the medicine-men of the Cherokee would not allow snakes to be killed. The Apache will not let snakes be killed within the limits of the camp by one of their own people, but they will not only allow a stranger to kill them, but request him to do so. They made this request of me on three occasions.

Several of the most influential medicine-men whom I have known were blind, among others old Na-ta-do-tash, whose medicine hat figures in these pages. Whether this blindness was the result of old age or due to the frenzy of dancing until exhausted in all seasons I am unable to conjecture.

Dunbar tells us that the medicine-men of the Pawnee swallowed arrows and knives, and had also the trick of apparently killing a man and bringing him back to life. The same power was claimed by the medicine-men of the Zuñi, and the story told me by old Pedro Pino of the young men whom they used to kill and restore to life, will be found in *The Snake Dance of the Moquis*.

The *materia medica* of the Apache is at best limited and comprehends scarcely anything more than roots, leaves, and other vegetable matter. In gathering these remedies they resort to no superstitious ceremonies that I have been able to detect, although I have not often seen them collecting. They prefer incantation to pharmacy at all times, although the squaws of the Walapai living near old Camp Beale Springs in 1873, were extremely fond of castor oil, for which they would beg each day.

The main reliance for nearly all disorders is the sweat bath, which is generally conducive of sound repose. All Indians know the benefit to be derived from relieving an overloaded stomach, and resort to the titillation of the fances with a feather to induce nausea. I have seen the Zuñi take great drafts of lukewarm water and then practice the above as a remedy in dyspepsia.

When a pain has become localized and deep seated, the medicine-men resort to suction of the part affected, and raise blisters in that way. I was once asked by the Walapai chief, Seqnanya, to look at his back and sides. He was covered with *cicatrices* due to such treatment, the medicine-men thinking thus to alleviate the progressive paralysis from which he had been long a sufferer, and from which he shortly afterwards died. After a long march, I have seen Indians of different bands expose the small of the back uncovered to the fierce heat of a pile of embers to produce a rubefacient effect and stimulate what is known as a weak back. They drink freely of hot teas or infusions of herbs and grasses for the cure of chills. They are all dextrous in the manufacture of splints out of willow twigs, and seem to meet with much success in their treatment of gunshot wounds, which they do not dress as often as white practitioners, alleging that the latter, by so frequently removing the bandages, unduly irritate the wounds. I have known them to apply *moxa*, and I remember to have seen two deep scars upon the left hand of the great Apache chief Cochise, due to this cause.

It should not be forgotten that the world owes a large debt to the medicine-men of America, who first discovered the virtues of coca, sarsaparilla, jalap, cinchona, and guiacum. They understand the administration of *enemata*, and have an apparatus made of the paunch of a sheep and the hollow leg bone.

Scarification is quite common, and is used for a singular purpose. The Apache scouts when tired were in the habit of sitting down and lashing their legs with bunches of nettles until the blood flowed. This,

27

according to their belief, relieved the exhaustion.

The medicine-men of the Floridians, according to Vaca, sucked and blew on the patient, and put hot stones on his abdomen to take away pain; they also scarified, and they seemed to have used *moxas*.

The medicine-men of Hispaniola cured by suction, and when they had extracted a stone or other alleged cause of sickness it was preserved as a sacred relic, especially by the women, who looked upon it as of great aid in parturition. Venegas speaks of a tube called the "*chacuaco*," formed out of a very hard black stone, used by the medicine-men of California in sucking such parts of the patient's body as were grievously afflicted with pains. In these tubes they sometimes placed lighted tobacco and blew down upon the part affected after the manner of a *moxa*, I suppose.

The men of Panuco were so addicted to drunkenness that we are told:

> *Lorsqu'ils sont fatigués de boire leur vin par la bouche, ils se couchent, élèvent les jambes en l'air, et s'en font introduire dans le fondement au moyen d'une canule, tant que le corps peut en coutenir.* (When they are tired of drinking their wine through the mouth, they lie down, elevate their legs in the air, and introduce it through a canula into the body cavity.)

The administration of wine in this manner may have been as a medicine, and the Aztecs of Panuco may have known that nutriment could be assimilated in this way. It shows at least that the Aztecs were acquainted with *enemata*.

Smith says that the medicine-men of the Araucanians "are well acquainted with the proper use of emetics, cathartics, and sudorifics. For the purpose of injection they make use of a bladder, as is still commonly practiced among the Chilenos."

Oviedo says of the medicine-men: "*Conoçian muchas hierbas de que usaban y eran apropiadas á diversas enfermedades.*"(I knew many herbs that were used and were appropriate to various diseases.)

One of the most curious remedies presented in Bancroft's first volume is the use of a poultice of mashed poison-ivy leaves as a remedy for ringworm by the Indians of Lower California.

The Indians of Topia (in the Sierra Madre, near Sinaloa), were in the habit of scarifying their tired legs and aching temples. The Arawaks, of Guiana, also scarified, according to Spencer. The inhabitants of Kamchatka use *enemata* much in the same way as the Navajo and Apache do. They also use *moxa* made of a fungus.

It has never been my good fortune to notice an example of tre-phining among our savage tribes, although I have seen a good many wounded, some of them in the head.

Dr. Fordyce Grinnell, who was for some years attached to the Wi-chita Agency as resident physician, has published the results of his observations in a monograph, entitled "The healing art as practiced by the Indians of the Plains," in which he says:

> Wet cupping is resorted to quite frequently. The surface is scari-fied by a sharp stone or knife, and a buffalo horn is used as the cupping glass. Cauterizing with red-hot irons is not infre-quently employed.

Smith says a cautery of "burning pith" was used by the Arauca-nians.

Dr. Edwin G. Meek says:

> It may be safely affirmed that a majority of the nation Choctaw prefer to receive the attentions of a white physician when one can be obtained. . . . . .When the doctor is called to his patient he commences operations by excluding all white men and all who disbelieve in the efficacy of his incantations.
> The [Apache] scouts seem to prefer their own medicine-men when seriously ill, and believe the weird singing and praying around the couch is more effective than the medicine dealt out by our camp 'sawbones.'[21]

The promptness with which the American Indian recovers from severe wounds has been commented upon by many authorities. From my personal observation I could, were it necessary, adduce many ex-amples. The natives of Australia seem to be endowed with the same recuperative powers.

After all other means have failed the medicine-men of the South-west devote themselves to making altars in the sand and clay near the couch of the dying, because, as Antonio Besias explained, this act was all the same as extreme unction. They portray the figures of various animals, and then take a pinch of the dust or ashes from each one and rub upon the person of the sick man as well as upon themselves. This matter of sand altars has been fully treated by Matthews in the report

---

21. Lieut. Pettit in *Jour. U. S. Mil. Serv. Instit.*, 1886.

of the Bureau of Ethnology for 1883-'84, and there are several representations to be found in my *Snake Dance of the Moquis*. Padre Boscana represents the "*puplem*" or medicine-men of the Indians of California as making or sketching "a most uncouth and ridiculous figure of an animal on the ground," and presumably of sands, clays, and other such materials.

<h3 style="text-align:center">HAIR AND WIGS.</h3>

The medicine-men of the Apache were, at least while young, extremely careful of their hair, and I have, often seen those who were very properly proud of their long and glossy *chevelure*. Particularly do I recall to mind the "doctor" at San Carlos in 1885, who would never allow his flowing black tresses to be touched. But they do not roach their hair, as I have seen the Pawnee do; they do not add false hair to their own, as I have seen among the Crow of Montana and the Mohave of the Rio Colorado; they do not apply plasters of mud as do their neighbours the Yuma, Cocopa, Mohave and Pima, and in such a manner as to convince spectators that the intent was ceremonial; and they do not use wigs in their dances. Wigs made of black wool may still be found occasionally among the Pueblos, but the Apache do not use them, and there is no reference to such a thing in their myths.

It is to be understood that these paragraphs are not treating upon the superstitions concerning the human hair, as such, but simply of the employment of wigs, which would seem in former days among some of the tribes of the Southwest to have been made of human hair presented by patients who had recovered from sickness or by mourners whose relatives had died.[22]

Some of the Apache-Yuma men wear long rolls of matted hair behind, which are the thickness of a finger, and two feet or more in length, and composed of old hair mixed with that growing on the head, or are in the form of a wig, made of hair that has been cut off when mourning the dead, to be worn on occasions of ceremony.

Sir Samuel Baker describes the peculiar wigs worn by the tribes on Lake Albert Nyanza, formed of the owner's hair and contributions from all sources plastered with clay into a stiff mass.

The Assinaboine used to wear false hair, and also had the custom of dividing their hair into "joints" of an inch or more, marked by a sort of paste of red earth and glue. The Mandan did the same. In this they

---

22. The "*pelucas*" mentioned of the Orinoco tribes by Padre Gumilla would seem to be nothing more than feather head-dresses.

both resemble the Mohave of the Rio Colorado. "The Algonquins believed also in a malignant Manitou. . . . . . She wore a robe made of the hair of her victims, for she was the cause of death."

The Apache, until within the last twenty years, (as at time of first publication), plucked out the eyelashes and often the eyebrows, but only a few of them still persist in the practice. Kane says that the Winnebagoes "have the custom of pulling out their eyebrows." Herrera says that among the signs by which the Tlascaltees recognized their gods when they saw them in visions, were *"vianle sin cejas, i sin pestañas,"* (with no eyebrows and no eyelashes.)

MUDHEADS.

Reference has been made to a ceremonial plastering of mud upon the heads of Indians. When General Crook was returning from his expedition into the Sierra Madre, Mexico, in 1883, in which expedition a few of the enemy had been killed, the scouts upon reaching the San Bernardino River made a free use of the sweat bath, with much singing and other formulas, the whole being part of the lustration which all warriors must undergo as soon as possible after being engaged in battle. The Apache proper did not apply mud to their heads, but the Apache-Yuma did.

Capt. Grossman, V. S. Army, says of the Pima method of purification after killing an Apache, that the isolation of the warrior lasts for sixteen days, during which period no one speaks to him, not even the old woman who brings him his food. The first day he touches neither food nor drink, and he eats sparingly for the whole time, touching neither meat nor salt; he bathes frequently in the Gila River and nearly the whole time keeps his head covered with a plaster of mud and *mesquite.*

> The boyes [of the Massagueyes] of seven or eight yeeres weare clay fastned on the hayre of the head, and still renewed with new clay, weighing sometimes five or six pounds. Nor may they be free hereof till in warre or lawfull fight hee hath killed a man.

According to Padre Geronimo Boscana, the traditions of the Indians of California show that they "fed upon a kind of clay." But this clay was often plastered upon their heads "as a kind of ornament." These were the Indians of San Juan Capistrano, who strongly resembled the Mohave. After all, the "mudheads" of the Mohave are no worse than

31

those people in India who still, (as at time of first publication), bedaub their heads with "the holy mud of the Ganges." Up to this time the mud has been the "blue mud " of the Colorado and other rivers, but when we find Herbert Spencer mentioning that the heads of the Comanche are "besmeared with a dull red clay" we may suspect that we have stumbled upon an analogue of the custom of the Aztec priests, who bedaubed their heads with the coagulating lifeblood of their human victims.

We know that there has been such a substitution practiced among the Indians of the Pueblo of Jemez, who apply red ochre to the mouth of the stone mountain lion, in whose honour human blood was once freely shed. The practice of so many of the Plains tribes of painting the median line of the head with vermilion seems to be traceable back to a similar custom.

SCALP SHIRTS.

The shirt depicted, made of buckskin and trimmed with human scalps, would seem to belong to the same category with the mantles made of votive hair, mentioned as being in use among the California tribe a little more than a century ago. It was presented to me by Little Big Man, who led me to believe that it had once belonged to the great chief of the Sioux, Crazy Horse, or had at least been worn by him. Of its symbolism I am unable to find the explanation. The colours yellow and blue would seem to represent the earth and water or sky, the feathers attached would refer to the birds, and the round circle on the breast is undoubtedly the sun. There is a cocoon affixed to one shoulder, the significance of which I do not know.

THE RHOMBUS, OR BULL ROARER.

The rhombus was first seen by me at the snake dance of the Tusayan, in the village of Walpi, Ariz., in the month of August, 1881. Previous to that date I had heard of it vaguely, but had never been able to see it in actual use. The medicine-men twirled it rapidly, and with a uniform motion, about the head and from front to rear, and succeeded in faithfully imitating the sound of a gust of rain-laden wind. As explained to me by one of the medicine-men, by making this sound they compelled the wind and rain to come to the aid of the crops. At a later date I found it in use among the Apache, and for the same purpose. The season near the San Carlos Agency during the year 1884 had been unusually dry, and the crops were parched. The medicine-men arranged a procession, two of the features of which were the

SHIRT OF THE "LITTLE BIG MAN" (SIOUX)

rhombus and a long handled cross, upon which various figures were depicted. Of the latter, I will speak at another time.

Again, while examining certain ruins in the Verde Valley, in central Arizona, I found that the "Cliff Dwellers," as it has become customary to call the prehistoric inhabitants, had employed the same weapon of persuasion in their intercourse with their gods. I found the rhombus also among the Rio Grande Pueblo tribes and the Zuñi. Dr. Washington Matthews has described it as existing among the Navajo and Maj. J. W. Powell has observed it in use among the Utes of Nevada and Utah. As will be shown, its use in all parts of the world seems to have been as general as that of any sacred implement known to primitive man, not even excepting the sacred cords or rosaries discussed in this paper.

Three forms of the rhombus have come under my own observation, each and all apparently connected in symbolism with the lightning. The first terminates in a triangular point, and the general shape is either that of a long, narrow, parallelogram, capped with an equilateral triangle, or else the whole figure is that of a slender isosceles triangle. Where the former shape was used, as at the Tusayan snake dance, the tracing of a snake or lightning in blue or yellow followed down the length of the rhombus and terminated in the small triangle, which did duty as the snake's head.

The second pattern was found by Dr. Matthews among the Navajo, and by myself in the old cliff dwellings. The one which I found was somewhat decayed, and the extremity of the triangle was broken off. There was no vestige of painting left. The second form was serrated on both edges to simulate the form of the snake or lightning. The third form, in use among the Apache, is an oblong of 7 or 8 inches in length, one and a quarter inches in width by a quarter in thickness. One extremity, that through which the cord passes, is rounded to rudely represent a human head, and the whole bears a close resemblance to the drawings of schoolboys which are intended for the human figure.

The Apache explained that the lines on the front side of the rhombus were the entrails and those on the rear side the hair of their wind god. The hair is of several colours, and represents the lightning. I did not ascertain positively that such was the case, but was led to believe that the rhombus of the Apache was made by the medicine-men from wood, generally pine or fir, which had been struck by lightning on the mountain tops. Such wood is held in the highest estimation

RHOMBUS OF THE APACHE.

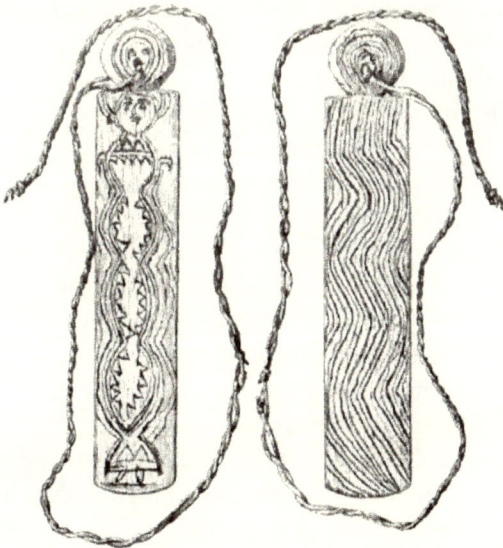

among them, and is used for the manufacture of amulets of especial efficacy. The Apache name for the rhombus is *tzi-ditindi*, the "sounding wood." The identification of the rhombus or "bull roarer" of the ancient Greeks with that used by the Tusayan in their snake dance was first made by E. B. Tylor in the *Saturday Review* in a criticism upon "The Snake Dance of the Moquis of Arizona."

THE CROSS.

The sign of the cross appears in many places in Apache symbolism. The general subject of the connection of the cross with the religion of the aborigines of the American continent has been so fully traversed by previous authors that I do not care to add much more to the subject beyond saying that my own observation has assured me that it is related to the cardinal points and the four winds, and is painted by warriors upon their moccasins upon going into a strange district in the hope of keeping them from getting on a wrong trail.

In October, 1884, I saw a procession of Apache men and women, led by the medicine-men bearing two crosses, made as follows: The vertical arm was 4 feet 10 inches long, and the transverse between 10 and 12 inches, and each was made of slats about 1½ inches wide, which looked as if they had been long in use. They were decorated with blue polka dots upon the unpainted surface.

A blue snake meandered down the longer arm. There was a circle of small willow twigs at top; next below that, a small zinc-cased mirror, a bell, and eagle feathers.

Nosey, the Apache whom I induced to bring it to me after the ceremony, said that they carried it in honour of Guzanutli to induce her to send rain, at that time much needed for their crops.

It is quite likely that this particular case represents a composite idea; that the original beliefs of the Apache have been modified to some extent by the crude ideas of the Mexican captives among them, who still remember much that was taught them in the churches of the hamlets in northern Mexico, from which they were kidnapped years ago; but, on the other hand, it is to be remembered that the cross has always formed a part of the Apache symbolism; that the snake does not belong to the Christian faith, and that it has never been allowed to appear upon the cross since the time of the Gnostics in the second and third centuries.

Therefore, we must regard that as a Pagan symbol, and so must we regard the circle of willow twigs, which is exactly the same as the circle we have seen attached to the sacred cords for the cure of headache.[23]

The cross was found in full vogue as a religious emblem among the aborigines all over America. Father Le Clercq speaks of its very general employment by the Gaspesiaus. He narrates that the Gaspé tradition or myth was, that the whole tribe being ravaged by a plague, the medicine men had recourse to the Sun, who ordered them to make use of the cross in every extremity.

NECKLACES OF HUMAN FINGERS.

The necklace of human fingers, an illustration of which accompanies this text, belonged to the foremost of the medicine-men of a brave tribe the Cheyenne of Montana and Wyoming. They were the backbone of the hostility to the whites, and during the long and arduous campaign conducted against them by the late Maj. Gen. George Crook, which terminated so successfully in the surrender of 4,500 of the allied Sioux and Cheyenne, at Red Cloud and Spotted Tail agencies, in the early spring of 1877, it was a noted fact that wherever a band of the Cheyenne was to be found there the fighting was most desperate. It is a matter now well established that the Cheyenne are an offshoot of the Aigouquian family, speaking a dialect closely resembling that of the Cree, of British America.

It may interest some readers to listen to a few words descriptive of the manner in which such a ghastly relic of savagery came into my possession. On the morning of the 25th of November. 1876, the cavalry and Indian scouts (Sioux, Shoshoni, Arapaho, Pawnee, and a few of the Cheyenne themselves), of Gen. Crook's command, under the leadership of the late Brig. Gen. Ranald S. Mackenzie, then colonel of the Fourth Cavalry, surprised and destroyed the main village of the Cheyenne, on the headwaters of the Powder River, in the Big Horn Mountains, Wyoming. The onslaught was irresistible, the destruction complete, and the discomfited savages were forced to flee from their beds, half naked and with nothing save their arms and ammunition.

More than half of the great herd of ponies belonging to the savages were killed, captured, or so badly wounded as to be of no use to the owners. The cold became so intense that on the night after the fight

23. "When the rain-maker of the Lenni Lennape would exert his power, he retired to some secluded spot and drew upon the earth the figure of a cross (its arms toward the cardinal points?), placed upon it a piece of tobacco, a gourd, a bit of some red stuff, and commenced to cry aloud to the spirits of the rains."—Brinton, *Myths of the New World*, (after Loskiel).

eleven *papooses* froze to death in their mothers' arms, and the succeeding night, three others. This blow, the most grievous ever inflicted upon the plains tribes, resulted in the surrender, first of the Cheyenne, and later on of the principal chief of the Sioux, the renowned Crazy Horse; after which the Sioux troubles were minimized into the hunt for scattered bands.

Undoubtedly, among the bitterest losses of valuable property suffered by the Cheyenne on this occasion were the two necklaces of human fingers which came into my possession, together with the small buckskin bag filled with the right hands of *papooses* belonging to the tribe of their deadly enemies, the Shoshoni. These were found in the village by one of our scouts—Baptiste Pourrier, who, with Mr. Frank Gruard, was holding an important and responsible position in connection with the care of the great body of Indian scouts already spoken of. From these two gentlemen I afterwards obtained all the information that is here to be found regarding the Cheyenne necklace.

The second necklace, consisting of four fingers, was buried, as Gen. Crook did not wish to have kept more than one specimen, and that only for scientific purposes. Accordingly, the necklace here depicted was sent first to the U. S. Military Academy at West Point, New York, and later to the National Museum in Washington, where it was believed it could better fulfil its mission of educating students in a knowledge of the manners and customs of our aborigines.

The buckskin bag, with the *papooses'* hands, was claimed by the Shoshoni scouts, who danced and wailed all night, and then burned the fearful evidence of the loss sustained by their people.

The necklace is made of a round collar of buckskin, incrusted with the small blue and white beads purchased from the traders, these being arranged in alternate spaces of an inch or more in length. There are also attached numbers of the perforated *wampum* shell beads of native manufacture. Pendant from this collar are five medicine arrows, the exact nature of which, it was, of course, impossible to determine from the owner himself. Both Frank and Baptiste agreed that an arrow might become "medicine" either from having been shot into the person of the owner himself or into the body of an enemy, or even from having been picked up under peculiar circumstances. The owner, High Wolf or Tall Wolf, admitted as much after he had surrendered at the Red Cloud Agency and had made every effort to obtain the return of his medicine, which was this necklace.

The four medicine bags to be seen in the picture are worthy of

NECKLACE OF HUMAN FINGERS.

attention. They were carefully examined under a powerful glass by Dr. H. C. Yarrow, U. S. Army, in the city of Washington, and pronounced to be human *scrota*. The first of these contained a vegetable powder, somewhat decomposed, having a resemblance to *hoddentin*; the second was filled with *killikiunick*; the third with small garnet-coloured seeds like the *chia* in use among the Apache, and the fourth with a yellow, clayey-white vegetable matter not identified. The fifth, also, remained unidentified.

Besides the above, there are artificial teeth, resembling those of the fossil animals abundant in the Bad Lands of South Dakota, but cut out of soft stone.

The fingers—eight altogether—are the left-hand middle fingers of Indians of hostile tribes, killed by High Wolf. I obtained the list and could insert it here were it worthwhile to do so. The fingers have not been left in the natural state, but have been subjected to very careful and elaborate antiseptic treatment in order thoroughly to desiccate them. They were split longitudinally on the inner side and after the bone had been extracted the surface of the skin, both inside and out, received a treatment with a wash or paint of ocherous earth, the same as is used for the face. I was told that the bones were not replaced but that sticks were inserted to maintain the fingers in proper shape.

Of the reason for making use of such a trophy or relic, there is not much to be said; even the savages know little and say less. From the best information that I have been able to gather, it would seem to be based partly upon a vainglorious desire to display the proofs of personal prowess, and partly upon the vague and ill defined, but deeply rooted, belief in the talismanic or " medicinal" potency possessed by all parts of the human body, especially after death. It was such a belief which impelled the Mandan, Aztecs, and others of the American tribes to preserve the skulls of their dead as well as (among the Aztecs) those of the victims sacrificed in honour of their gods. As has been shown in another place, the Zuñi and others take care to offer food at stated periods to the scalps of their enemies.

The use of necklaces of human fingers or of human teeth is to be found in many parts of the world, and besides the fingers themselves, we find the whole arm, or in other cases only the nails. The Cheyenne did not always restrict themselves to fingers; they generally made use of the whole hand, or the arm of the slaughtered enemy. In a coloured picture drawn and painted by one of themselves I have a representation of a scalp dance, in which the squaws may be seen dressed in their best, earring the arms of enemies elevated on high poles and lances. There is no doubt in my mind that this custom of the Cheyenne of cutting off the arm or hand gave rise to their name in the sign language of the "Slashers," or "Wrist Cutters," much as the corresponding tribal peculiarity of the Dakota occasioned their name of the "Coupe Gorge" or "Throat Cutters."

The necklace of human fingers is found among other tribes. A necklace of four human fingers was seen by the members of the Lewis and Clarke expedition among the Shoshoni at the headwaters of the Columbia, in the early years of the present century. Early in the spring of 1838 Henry Youle Hind refers to the allies of the Ojibwa on Red River as having "two fingers severed from the hands of the unfortunate Sioux."

In Eastman's *Legends of the Sioux*, we read of "Harpsthinah, one of the Sioux women, who wore as long as she could endure it, a necklace made of the hands and feet of Chippewah children." We read that in New Zealand, "Several rows of human teeth, drawn on a thread, hung on their breasts." Capt. Cook speaks of seeing fifteen human jaw bones attached to a semicircular board at the end of a long house on the island of Tahiti. "They appeared to be fresh, and there was not one of them that wanted a single tooth;" and also, "the model of a canoe, about three feet long, to which were tied eight human jaw bones; we had already learnt that these were trophies of war." Capt. Byron, R. N., saw in the Society Islands, in 1765, a chief who "had a string of human teeth about his waist, which was probably a trophy of his military prowess."

> The wild Andamanese, who live only on the fruits of their forests and on fish, so far revere their progenitors that they adorn their women and children with necklaces and such like, formed out of the finger and toe-nails of their ancestors.—Forlong, *Rivers of Life,* vol. 1.

Bancroft says that the Californians did not generally scalp, but they did cut off and keep the arms and legs of a slain enemy or, rather, the hands and feet and head. They also had the habit of plucking out and preserving the eyes.

Kohl assures us that he has been informed that the Ojibwa will frequently cut fingers, arms, and limbs from their enemies and preserve these ghastly relics for use in their dances. Sometimes the warriors will become so excited that they will break off and swallow a finger.

Tanner says of the Ojibwa: "Sometimes they use sacks of human skin to contain their medicines, and they fancy that something is thus added to their efficacy."

Of the savages of Virginia we read, (quoting Capt. John Smith):

Mais d'autres portent pour plus glorieuse parure une main seiche de quelqu'un de leurs ennemis, (But others are carry a more glorious adornment a hand of someone of their enemies.)

Of the Algonkin we read in *Jesuit Relations*:

Il y en a qui ont une partie du bras et la main de quelque Hiroquois qu'ils out tué; cela est si bien vuidée que les ongles resteut toutes en-tieres. So the nails remain whole.

The Mohawk we read in the *Third Voyage of David Peter De Vries* :

. . . . . place their foe against a tree or stake and first tear all the nails from his fingers and run them on a string, which they wear the same as we do gold chains. It is considered to the honour of any chief who has vanquished or overcome his enemies if he bite off or cut off some of their members, as whole fingers.

The Cenis (Asinai) of Texas, were seen by La Salle's expedition in 1687-1690, torturing a captive squaw. "They then tore out her hair, and cut off her fingers.'"

In the *Army and Navy Journal*, New York, June 23, 1888, is mentioned a battle between the Crow of Montana and the Piegan, in which the former obtained some of the hands and feet of dead warriors of the first-named tribe and used them in their dances.

Catlin shows that the young Sioux warriors, after going through the ordeal of the sun dance, placed the little finger of the left hand on the skull of a sacred buffalo and had it chopped off.

"The sacrifices [of American Indians] at the fasts at puberty sometimes consist of finger joints." (Frazer, *Totemism*)

In Dodge's *Wild Indians* is represented a Cheyenne necklace of the bones of the first joint of the human fingers, stripped of skin and flesh. I have never seen or heard of anything of the kind, although I have served with the Cheyenne a great deal and have spoken about their customs. My necklace is of human fingers mummified, not of bones.

Fanny Kelly says of a Sioux chief:

He showed me a puzzle or game he had made from the finger bones of some of the victims that had fallen beneath his own tomahawk. The bones had been freed from the flesh by boiling, and, being placed upon a string, were used for playing some kind of Indian game.—*My Captivity Among the Sioux Indians by* Fanny Kelly,(also published by Leonaur).

The use of dead men's toes, fingers, spinal vertebrae, etc., in magical ceremonies, especially the fabrication of magical lamps and candles, is referred to by Frommann.

NECKLACES OF HUMAN TEETH.

A number of examples are to be found of the employment of necklaces of human teeth. In my own experience I have never come across any specimens, and my belief is that among the Indians south of the Isthmus such things are to be found almost exclusively. I have found no reference to such ornamentation or "medicine" among the tribes of North America, but there are many to show the very general dissemination of the custom in Africa and in the islands of the South Sea. Gomara says that the Indians of Santa Marta wore at their necks, like dentists, the teeth of the enemies they had killed in battle.

Among some of the Australian tribes the women wear about their necks the teeth which have been knocked out of the mouths of the boys at a certain age. This custom of the Australians does not obtain among the North American tribes, by whom the teeth, as they fall out, are carefully hidden or buried under some tree or rock. At least, I have been so informed by several persons, among others by Chato, one of the principal men of the Chiricahua Apache.

Molina speaks of the customs of the Araucanians, who, after torturing their captives to death, made war flutes out of their bones and used the skulls for drinking vessels.

THE SCRATCH STICK.

When Gen. Crook's expedition against the Chiricahua Apache reached the heart of the Sierra Madre,[24] Mexico, in 1883, it was my good fortune to find on the ground in Geronimo's *rancheria* two insignificant looking articles of personal equipment, to which I learned the Apache attached the greatest importance. One of these was a very small piece of hard wood, cedar, or pine, about two and a half to three inches long and half a finger in thickness, and the other a small section of the cane indigenous to the Southwest and of about the same

---

24. *On the Border With Crook* and *An Apache Campaign in the Sierra Madre* by John G. Bourke also published by Leonaur.

dimensions. The first was the scratch stick and the second the drinking reed.

The rule enjoined among the Apache is that for the first four times one of their young men goes out on the warpath he must refrain from scratching his head with his fingers or letting water touch his lips. How to keep this vow and at the same time avoid unnecessary personal discomfort and suffering is the story told by these petty fragments from the Apache's ritual. He does not scratch his head with his fingers; he makes use of this scratch stick. He will not let water touch his lips, but sucks it into his throat through this tiny tube. A long leather cord attached both stick and reed to the warrior's belt and to each other. This was all the information I was able to obtain of a definite character.

Whether these things had to be prepared by the medicine-men or by the young warrior himself; with what ceremonial, if any, they had to be manufactured, and under what circumstances of time and place, I was unable to ascertain to my own satisfaction, and therefore will not extend my remarks or burden the student's patience with incoherent statements from sources not absolutely reliable. That the use of the scratch stick and the drinking reed was once very general in America and elsewhere, and that it was not altogether dissociated from ritualistic or ceremonial ideas, may be gathered from the citations appended.

In her chapter entitled "Preparatory ceremony of the young warrior" Mrs. Emerson says: "He does not touch his ears or head with his hand," explaining in a foot note, "the head was sometimes made a sacrificial offering to the sun." Tanner relates that the young Ojibwa warrior for the "three first times" that he accompanies a war party "must never scratch his head or any other part of his body with his fingers, but if he is compelled to scratch he must use a small stick."

Kohl states that the Ojibwa, while on the warpath, "will never sit down in the shade of a tree or scratch their heads; at least, not with their fingers. The warriors, however, are permitted to scratch themselves with a piece of wood or a comb." Mackenzie states regarding the Indians whom he met on the Columbia, in 52 38', N. lat., "instead of a comb they [the men] have a small stick hanging by a string from one of the locks [of hair], which they employ to alleviate any itching or irritation in the head."

The Tlinkit of British North America use these scratchers made of basalt or other stone.

"The pipe stem carrier (*i. e.,* the carrier of the sacred or 'medicine' pipe) of the Crees, of British North America, dares not scratch his own head, without compromising his own dignity, without the intervention of a stick, which he always carries for that purpose."(Kane, *Wanderings of an Artist in North America*).

Bancroft quotes Walker as saying that "a Pima never touches his skin with his nails, but always with a small stick for that purpose, which he renews every fourth day and wears in his hair."

As part of the ceremony of "initiating youth into manhood" among the Creeks, the young neophyte "during the twelve moons is also forbidden to pick his ears or scratch his head with his fingers, but must use a small splinter to perform these operations." (Hawkins in *Legend of the Creeks*, Gatschet.)

The Apache-Yuma men carry in their hair "a slender stick or bone about 8 inches long, which serves them as a comb." (Corbusier, *American Antiquarian*.)

The idea that these scratch sticks replace combs is an erroneous one; Indians make combs in a peculiar way of separate pieces of wood, and they are also very fond of brushing their long locks with the coarse brushes, which they make of *sacaton* or other grass.

"One other regulation, mentioned by Schomburgk, is certainly quaint; the interesting father may not scratch himself with his finger nails, but may use for this purpose a splinter, especially provided, from the mid-rib of a *cokerite* palm."

Alarcon, describing the tribes met on the Rio Colorado, in 1541, says:

"They weare certaine pieces of Deeres bones fastened to their armes, wherewith they strike off the sweate." (Hakluyt, *Voyages*).

Thus far, the suggestion of a religious or ceremonial idea attaching to the custom of scratching has not been apparent, unless we bear in mind that the warrior setting out on the warpath never neglects to surround himself with all the safeguards which the most potent incantations and "medicine" of every kind can supply. But Herbert Spencer tells us in two places that the Creeks attach the idea of a ceremonial observance to the custom. He says that "the warriors have a ceremony of scratching each other as a sign of friendship;" and again, "scratching is practiced among young warriors as a ceremony or token of friendship. When they have exchanged promises of inviolable attachment, they proceed to scratch each other before they part."

Dr. J. Hampden Porter remarks that this ceremonial scratching may be a "survival" of the blood covenant, and that in earlier times the young warriors, instead of merely scratching each other's arms, may have cut the flesh and exchanged the blood. The idea seems to be a very sensible one.

Father Alegre describes a ceremonial scratching which may have been superseded by the scratch stick, to which the medicine-men of certain tribes subjected the young men before they set out on the warpath. Among the Pima and Opata the medicine-men drew from their quivers the claws of eagles, and with these gashed the young man along the arms from the shoulders to the wrists.

This last paragraph suggests so strongly certain of the practices at the sun dance of the tribes farther to the north that it may be well to compare it with the other allusions in this paper to that dance.

It will be noticed that the use of the scratch-stick, at least among the tribes of America, seems to be confined to the male sex; but the information is supplied by Mr. Henshaw, of the Bureau of Ethnology, that the Indians of Santa Barbara, Cal., made their maidens at the time of attaining womanhood wear pendant from the neck a scratcher of abalone shell, which they had to use for an indefinite period when the scalp became irritable.

Prof. Otis T. Mason, of the National Museum, informs me that there is a superstition in Virginia to the effect that a young woman *enciente* for the first time must, under no circumstances, scratch her head with her fingers, at least while uncovered; she must either put on gloves or use a small stick.

The Parsi have a festival at which they serve a peculiar cake or bread called "*draona*," which is marked by scratches from the finger nails of the woman who has baked it.[25]

No stress has been laid upon the appearance in all parts of the world of "back scratchers" or "scratch my backs," made of ivory, bone, or wood, and which were used for toilet purposes to remove irritation from between the shoulder blades or along the spine where the hand itself could not reach.

The Drinking Reed.

Exactly what origin to ascribe to the drinking reed is now an impossibility, neither is it probable that the explanations which the medicine-men might choose to make would have the slightest value

---

25. When the "*drôn*" has been marked with three rows of finger-nail scratches it is called a "*frasast*."

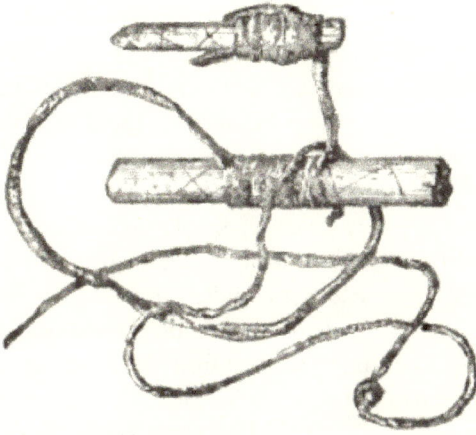

THE SCRATCH STICK AND DRINKING REED

in dispelling the gloom which surrounds the subject. That the earliest conditions of the Apache tribe found them without many of the comforts which have for generations been necessaries, and obliged to resort to all sorts of expedients in cooking, carrying, or serving their food is the most plausible presumption, but it is submitted merely as a presumption and in no sense as a fact.

It can readily be shown that in a not very remote past the Apache and other tribes were compelled to use bladders and reeds for carrying water, or for conveying water, broth, and other liquid food to the lips. The conservative nature of man in all that involves his religion would supply whatever might be needed to make the use of such reeds obligatory in ceremonial observances wherein there might be the slightest suggestion of religious impulse. We can readily imagine that among a people not well provided with forks and spoons, which are known to have been of a much later introduction than knives, there would be a very decided danger of burning the lips with broth, or of taking into the mouth much earthy and vegetable matter or ice from springs and streams at which men or women might wish to drink, so the use of the drinking reed would obviate no small amount of danger and discomfort.

The manner in which the natives of the New Hebrides and other islands of the South Pacific Ocean carry water in bamboo joints recalls the Zuñi method of preserving the sacred water of the ocean in hollow reeds.

"The Malabars reckoned it insolent to touch the vessel with their lips when drinking." They made use of vessels with a spout, which were no more and no less than the small hollow-handled soup ladles of the Zuñi and Tusayan, through which they sipped their hot broth.

Alarcon relates that the tribes seen on the Rio Colorado by him in 1541, wore on one arm "certain small pipes of cane." But the object or purpose of wearing these is not indicated.

Mrs. Ellen Russell Emerson speaks of the custom the warriors of the northern tribes had which suggests that she had heard of the drinking reed without exactly understanding what it meant. She says that warriors carry bowls of birch bark "from one side of which the warrior drinks in going to battle—from the other, on his return. These bowls are not carried home, but left on the prairie, or suspended from trees within a, day's journey of his village."

There was another service performed by reeds or tubes in the domestic economy of nations around the north pole. As the Apache are derived from an Arctic ancestry it does not seem amiss to allude to it. Lord Lonsdale, in describing the capture of a whale which he witnessed, says that the Eskimo women "first of all gathered up the harpoons and then pulled out all the spears. As each spear was withdrawn a blow pipe was pushed into the wound and the men blew into it, after which the opening was tied up. When every wound had been treated in this manner the whale resembled a great windbag and floated high in the water."

In the National Museum at Washington, D. C., there are many pipes made of the bones of birds, which were used by the limit as drinking tubes when water had to be taken into the mouth from holes cut in the ice. These drinking tubes seem to be directly related to our subject, although they may also have been used as Lonsdale describes the pipes for blowing the dead whale full of air. Another point to be mentioned is that the eagle pipe kept in the mouth of the young warrior undergoing the torture of the sun dance among the Sioux and other tribes on the plains is apparently connected with the "*bebedero del Sol*" of the peoples to the south.

The use of this drinking reed, shown to have been once so intimately associated with human sacrifice, may have disappeared upon the introduction of labrets, which seem, in certain cases at least, to be associated with the memory of enemies killed in battle, which would be only another form of human sacrifice. This suggestion is advanced with some misgivings, and only as a hypothesis to assist in determining for what purpose labrets and drinking tubes have been employed.

The Apache have discontinued the use of the labret, which still is to be found among their congeners along the Lower Yukon, but not among those living along the lower river. According to Dall the custom was probably adopted from the Inuit; he also shows that whenever labrets are worn in a tribe they are worn by both sexes, and that the women assume them at the first appearance of the *catamenia*.

> This is to be noted, that how many men these Savages [Brazilians] doe kill, so many holes they will have in their visage, beginning first in their nether lippe, then in their cheekes, thirdly, in both their eye-browes, and lastly in their eares.—Peter Carder, an Englishman captive among the Brazilians. 1578-1586. in *Purchas*, vol. 4.

Cabeza de Vaca speaks of the Indians near Malhado Island, "They likewise have the nether lippe bored, and within the same they carrie a piece of thin cane about halfe a finger thicke."

Herrera relates very nearly the same of the men of "Florida": "*Traìan una tetilla oradada, metido por el agujero un pedaço de caña, i el labio baxero tambien agujereado, con otra caña en èl.*" But Herrera probably obtained his data from the narrative of Vaca.

In looking into this matter of labrets as connected or suspected as being in some way connected with the drinking reed, we should not expect to find the labret adhering very closely to the primitive form, because the labret, coming to be regarded more and more as an ornament, would allow greater and greater play to the fancy of the wearer or manufacturer, much the same as the crosses now worn by ladies, purely as matter of decoration, have become so thoroughly examples of dexterity in *filagree* work as to have lost the original form and significance as a declaration of faith.

Hoddentin and the
Pollen of the Tule

Trifles not infrequently lead to important results. In every walk of science a trifle disregarded by incurious thousands has repaid the inquisitiveness of a single observer with unhoped-for knowledge.—Dean, *Serpent Worship.*

The taciturnity of the Apache in regard to all that concerns their religious ideas is a very marked feature of their character; probably no tribe with which our people have come in contact has succeeded more thoroughly in preserving from profane inquiry a complete knowledge of matters relating to their beliefs and ceremonials. How much of this ignorance is to be attributed to interpreters upon whom reliance has necessarily been placed, and how much to the indisposition of the Apache to reveal anything concerning himself, it would be fruitless to inquire, but, in my own experience, when I first went among them in New Mexico and Arizona twenty-three years ago, I was foolish enough to depend greatly upon the Mexican captives who had lived among the Apache since boyhood, and who might be supposed to know exactly what explanation to give of every ceremony in which the Apache might engage.

Nearly every one of these captives, or escaped captives, had married among the Apache, and had raised families of half-breed children, and several of them had become more Apache than the Apache themselves. Yet I was time and again assured by several of these interpreters that the Apache had no religion, and even after I had made some progress in my investigations, at every turn I was met by the most contradictory statements, due to the interpreter's desire to inject his own views and not to give a frank exposition of those submitted by the Apache. Thus, an Apache god would be transmuted into either a "*santo*" or a "*diablo*," according to the personal bias of the Mexican who happened to be assisting me. "*Assanutlije*" assumed the disguise of "*Maria Santissima*," while ceremonies especially sacred and beneficent in the eyes of the savages were stigmatized as "*brujeria*" and "*hechiceria*" (witchcraft) in open defiance of the fact that the Apache have as much horror and dread of witches as the more enlightened of their brethren who in past ages suffered from their machinations in Europe and America.

The interpreters had no intention to deceive; they were simply unable to disengage themselves from their own prejudices and their own ignorance; they could not, and they would not, credit the existence of any such thing as religion, save and excepting that taught them at their mothers' knees in the petty hamlets of Sonora and of which they still preserved hazy and distorted recollections. One of the first things to be noticed among the Apache, in this connection, was the very general appearance of little bags of buckskin, sometimes ornamented, sometimes plain, which were ordinarily attached to the belts of the warriors, and of which they seemed to be especially careful. [1]

What follows in this chapter was not learned in an hour or a day, but after a long course of examination and a comparison of statements extracted from different authorities.

The bags spoken of revealed when opened a quantity of yellow coloured flour or powder, resembling cornmeal, to which the Apache gave the name of "*hoddentin*," or "*hadntin*," the meaning of which word is "the powder or pollen of the *tule*," a variety of the cat-tail rush, growing in all the little ponds and *cienegas* of the Southwest.

I made it the touchstone of friendship that every scout or other Apache who wished for a favour at my hands should relate something concerning his religious belief. I did not care much what topic he selected; it might be myths, clan laws, war customs, medicine— anything he pleased, but it had to be something and it had to be accurate. *Hoddentin* having first attracted my attention, I very naturally made many of my first inquiries about it, and, while neglecting no opportunity for independent observation, drew about me the most responsible men and women, heard what each had to say, carefully compared and contrasted it with the statements of the others, and now give the result.

I noticed that in the dances for the benefit of the sick the medi-

---

1. The medicine sack or bag of the Apache, containing their "*hoddentin*," closely resembles the "*bulla*" of the Romans. *Musée de Naples*. Copy shown me by Mr. Spofford, of the Library of Congress.

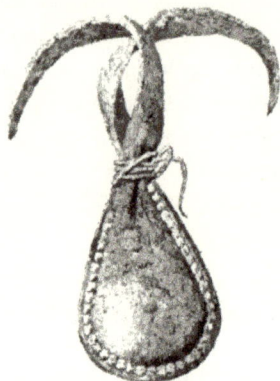

BAG CONTAINING HODDENTIN.

cine-men in the intervals between chants applied this yellow powder
to the forehead of the patient, then in form of a cross upon his breast,
then in a circle around his couch, then upon the heads of the chant-
ers and of sympathizing friends, and lastly upon their own heads and
into their own mouths. There is a considerable difference in method,
as medicine-men allow themselves great latitude, or a large "personal
equation," in all their dealings with the supernatural.

No Apache would, if it could be avoided, go on the warpath without a bag of this precious powder somewhere upon his person, generally, as I have said, attached to his ammunition belt. Whenever one
was wounded, hurt, or taken sick while on a scout, the medicine-man
of the party would walk in front of the horse or mule ridden by the
patient and scatter at intervals little pinches of *hoddentin*, that his path
might be made easier. As was said to me:

> When we Apache go on the warpath, hunt, or plant, we always
> throw a pinch of *hoddentin* to the sun, saying 'with the favour of
> the sun, or permission of the sun, I am going out to fight, hunt,
> or plan', as the case may be, 'and I want the sun to help me.'

> I have noticed that the Apache, when worn out with marching, put
a pinch of *hoddentin* on their tongues as a restorative.

> *Hoddentin* is eaten by sick people as a remedy. (Information
> from Tze-go-juni.)

> Before starting out on the warpath, they take a pinch of *hod-
> deutin*, throw it to the sun, and also put a pinch on their tongues
> and one on the crown of the head. . . . When they return, they

hold a dance, and on the morning of that day throw pinches of *hoddentin* to the rising sun, and then to the east, south, west, and north, to the four winds. (Information from Concepcion.)

I am unable to assert that *hoddentin* is used in any way at the birth of a child; but I know that as late as 1886 there was not a babe upon the San Carlos reservation, no matter how tender its age, that did not have a small bag of *hoddentin* attached to its neck or dangling from its cradle. Neither can I assert anything about its use at time of marriage, because, among the Apache, marriage is by purchase, and attended with little, if any, ceremony. But when an Apache girl attains the age of puberty, among other ceremonies performed upon her, they throw *hoddentin* to the sun and strew it about her and drop on her head flour of the *piñon*, which flour is called by the Chiricahua Apache "*nostchi*," and by the Sierra Blanca Apache "*opé*".[2]

Upon attaining the age of puberty, girls fast one whole day, pray, and throw *hoddentin* to the sun," (Tze-go-juni). When an Apache dies, if a medicine-man be near, *hoddentin* is sprinkled upon the corpse. The Apache buried in the clefts of rocks, but the Apache-Mohave cremated. "Before lighting the fire the medicine-men of the Apache-Mohave put *hoddentin* on the dead person's breast in the form of a cross, on the forehead, shoulders, and scattered a little about. (Mike Burns)

The very first thing an Apache does in the morning is to blow a little pinch of *hoddentin* to the dawn. The Apache worship both dawn and darkness, as well as the sun, moon, and several of the planets.

When the sun rises we cast a pinch of *hoddentin* toward him, and we do the same thing to the moon, but not to the stars, saying '*Gun-ju-le, chigo-na-ay, si-chi-zi, gun-ju-le, inzayu, ijanale,*' meaning 'Be good, O Sun, be good.' 'Dawn, long time let me live'; or, 'Don't let me die for a long time,' and at night, '*Gun-ju-le, chil-jilt, si-chi-zi, gun-ju-le, inzayu, ijanale,*' meaning 'Be good, O Night; Twilight, be good; do not let me die.' In going on a hunt an Apache throws *hoddentin* and says '*Gun-ju-le, chigo-na-ay, cha-ut-si, ping, kladitza,*' meaning 'Be good, O Sun, make me succeed deer to kill.' (Mickey Free)

The name of the full moon in the Apache language is "*klego-na-ay*,"

2. The word "*opé*" suggests the name the Tusuyan have for themselves, Opi, or Opika, "bread people."

but the crescent moon is called "*tzontzose*" and *hoddentin* is always offered to it. (Alchise, Mike, and others).

> *Hoddentin* is thrown to the sun, moon (at times), the morning star, and occasionally to the wagon. (Francesca and other captive Chiricahua squaws).

> The Apache offer much *hoddentin* to 'Na-n-kuzze,' the Great Bear. (Moses Henderson).

> Our custom is to throw a very small pinch of *hoddentin* at dawn to the rising sun. (Chato)

> The women of the Chiricahua throw no *hoddentin* to the moon, but pray to it, saying: "*Gun-ju-le, klego-na-ay,*" (be good, O Moon). (Tze-go-juni).

When the Apache plant corn the medicine-men bury eagle-plume sticks in the fields, scatter *hoddentin*, and sing. When the corn is partially grown they scatter pinches of *hoddentin* over it. (Moses Henderson and other Apache at san Carlos).

The "eagle-plume sticks" mentioned in the preceding paragraph suggests the "*ke-thawn*" mentioned by Matthews in *The Mountain Chant*. (Bureau of Ethnology, Report for 1883-'84).

> When a person is very sick the Apache make a great fire, place the patient near it, and dance in a circle around him and the fire, at the same time singing and sprinkling him with *hoddentin* in the form of a cross on head, breast, arms, and legs. (Francesca and others).

In November, 1885, while at the San Carlos agency, I had an interview with Nantadotash, an old blind medicine-man of the Akañe or Willow gens, who had with him a very valuable medicine-hat which he refused to sell, and only with great reluctance permitted me to touch. Taking advantage of his infirmity, I soon had a picture drawn in my notebook, and the text added giving the symbolism of all the ornamentation attached. Upon discovering this, the old man became much excited, and insisted upon putting a pinch of *hoddentin* upon the drawing, and then recited a prayer, which I afterwards succeeded in getting *verbatim*.

After the prayer was finished, the old man arose and marked with *hoddentin* the breast of his wife, of Moses, of Antonio, of other Apache present, and then of myself, putting a large pinch over my heart and upon each shoulder, and then placed the rest upon his own tongue. He explained that I had taken the "life" out of his medicine hat, and, notwithstanding the powers of his medicine, returned in less than a month with a demand for $30 as damages.

His hat never was the same after I drew it. My suggestion that the application of a little soap might wash away the clots of grease, soot, and earth adhering to the hat, and restore its pristine efficacy were received with the scorn due to the sneers of the scoffer.

In time of much lightning, the Apache throw *hoddentin* and say: '*Gun-ju-le, ittindi,*' be good, Lightning. (Tze-go-juni).

Tzit-jizinde, "the Man who likes Everybody," who said he belonged to the Inoschujochin—Manzanita or Bearberry clan showed me how to pray with *hoddentin* in time of lightning or storm or danger of any kind. Taking a small pinch in his fingers, he held it out at arm's length, standing up, and repeated his prayer, and then blew his breath hard. I was once with a party of Apache while a comet was visible. I called their attention to it, but they did not seem to care. On the other hand, Antonio told me that the "biggest dance" the Apache ever had was during the time that "the stars all fell out of the sky" (1833).

The only act of a religious character which I observed . . was shortly after crossing the river they [*i. e.,* the American officers] were met by a small party of the Indians, one of whom chalked a cross on the breast of each, with a yellow earth, which he carried in a satchel at his belt. Previous to doing so he muttered some words very solemnly with his hands uplifted and eyes thrown upwards. Again, on arriving at the camp of the people, the chief and others in greeting them took a similar vow, touching thereafter the yellow chalked cross. Sonora may have furnished them with some of their notions of a Deity.—Smart, *Smithsonian Report for 1867.*

"The yellow earth," seen by Dr. Smart was, undoubtedly, *hoddentin,* carried in a medicine bag at the belt of a medicine-man. Some years ago I went out with Al. Seiber and a small party of Apache to examine three of their "sacred caves" in the Sierra Pinal and Sierra Ancha. No better opportunity could have been presented for noting what they did. The very last thing at night they intoned a "medicine" song, and at early dawn they were up to throw a pinch of *hoddentin* to the east.

Moses and John, two of the Apache mentioned above, requested permission to go off in the mountains after deer and bear, supposed to be plentiful in the higher altitudes. Before leaving camp, Moses blew a pinch of *hoddentin* toward the sun, repeating his prayer for success, and ending it with a sharp, snappy "*ek,*" as if to call attention. In one of the sacred caves visited on this trip, the Apache medicine-men assembled for the purpose of holding their snake dance. This I have never seen among the Apache, but that they celebrate it and that it is fully the equal of the repulsive rite which I have witnessed and noted among the Tusayan I am fully assured. I may make reference to some of its features in the chapter upon animal worship and ophic rites.

From a multiplicity of statements, the following are taken: Concepcion had seen the snake dance over on the Carrizo, near Camp Apache; the medicine-men threw *hoddentin* upon the snakes. He said:

> After getting through with the snake, the medicine-man suffered it to glide off, covered with the *hoddentin,* thrown by admiring devotees.

Mike Burns had no remembrance of seeing *hoddentin* thrown to the sun. He had seen it thrown to the snake, "in a kind of worship."

Nott and Antonio stated that "when they find that a snake has wriggled across the trail, especially the trail to be followed by a war party, they throw *hoddentin* upon the trail." Nott took a pinch of *hoddeutin,* showed how to throw it upon the snake, and repeated the prayer, which I recorded.

Corbusier instances a remedy in use among the Tonto Apache. This consisted in applying a rattlesnake to the head or other part suffering from pain. He continues:

> After a time the medicine-man rested the snake on the ground again, and, still retaining his hold of it with his right hand, put a pinch of yellow pollen into its mouth with his left, and rubbed some along its belly.[3]

> He then held his hand out to a man, who took a pinch of the powder and rubbed it on the crown of a boy's head. Yellow pollen treated in this manner is a common remedy for headache, and may frequently be seen on the crowns of the heads of men and boys.

Hoddentin is used in the same manner as a remedy for headache

---

3. In the third volume of Kingsborough, on plate 17, an Aztec, probably a priest, is shown offering food to a snake, which eats it out of his hand.

among the San Carlos Apache, but the medicine-men apply a snake to the person of a patient only when their "diagnosis" has satisfied them that he has been guilty of some unkindness to a snake, such as stepping upon it, in which case they pretend that they can cure the man by applying to the part affected the portion of the reptile's body upon which he trampled.

The Apache state that when their medicine-men go out to catch snakes for their snake dance, they recite a prayer and lay their left hand, in which is some *hoddentin*, at the opening of the snake's den, through which the reptile must crawl, and, after a short time the snake will come out and allow himself to be handled.

Hoddentin is also offered to other animals, especially the bear, of which the Apache, like their congeners the Navajo, stand in great awe and reverence. When a bear is killed, the dance which is held becomes frenzied; the skin is donned by all the men, and much *hoddentin* is thrown, if it can be obtained. One of these dances which I saw in the Sierra Madre, Mexico, in 1883, lasted all night, without a moment's cessation in the singing and prancing of the participants.

A great deal of *hoddentin* is offered to the "*ka-chu*" (great or jack rabbit). (Information Moses Henderson)

The Apache medicine-man, Nakay-do-klunni, called by the whites "*Bobbydoklinny*," exercised great influence over his people at Camp Apache, in 1881. He boasted of his power to raise the dead, and predicted that the whites should soon be driven from the land. He also drilled the savages in a peculiar dance, the like of which had never been seen among them. The participants, men and women, arranged themselves in files, facing a common centre, like the spokes of a wheel, and while thus dancing *hoddentin* was thrown upon them in profusion. This prophet or "doctor" was killed in the engagement in the Cibicu Canyon, August 30, 1881.

In a description of the "altars" made by the medicine-men of the Apache-Yuma at or near Camp Verde, Arizona, it is shown that this sacred powder is freely used. Figures were drawn upon the ground to represent the deities of the tribe, and the medicine-men dropped on all, except three of them, a pinch of yellow powder (*hoddentin*) which was taken from a small buckskin bag. This powder was put upon the head, chest, or other part of the body of the patient.

Surgeon Corbusier, U. S. Army, says that the ceremony just described was "a most sacred one and entered into for the purpose of averting the diseases with which the Apache at Camp Verde had been afflicted the summer previous."

I am not sure that the Apache-Yuma have not borrowed the use of *hoddentin* from the Apache. My reason for expressing this opinion is that I have never seen an Apache without a little bag of *hoddentin* when it was possible for him to get it, whereas I have never seen an Apache-Yuma with it except when he was about to start out on the warpath. The "altars" referred to by Corbusier are made also by the Apache, Navajo, Zuñi, and Tusayan. Those of the Apache, as might be inferred from their nomadic state, were the crudest; those of the Navajo, Zuñi, and Tusayan display a wonderful degree of artistic excellence. The altars of the Navajo have been described and illustrated by Dr. Washington Matthews, and those of the Tusayan by myself.

Moses Henderson, wishing me to have a profitable interview with his father, who was a great snake doctor among the Apache, told me that when he brought him to see me I should draw two lines across each other on his right foot, and at their junction place a bead of the *chalchihuitl*, the cross to be drawn with *hoddentin*. The old man would then tell me all he knew.

The Apache, I learned, at times offer *hoddentin* to fire, an example of *pyrodulia* for which I had been on the lookout, knowing that the Navajo have fire dances, the Zuñi the Feast of the Little God of Fire, and the, Apache themselves are not ignorant of the fire dance.

Hoddentin seems to be used to strengthen all solemn compacts and to bind faith. I had great trouble with a very bright medicine-man named Na-a-cha, who obstinately refused to let me look at the contents of a phylactery which he constantly wore until I let him know that I, too, was a medicine-man of eminence. The room in which we had our conversation was the quarters of the post surgeon, at that time absent on scout. The chimney piece was loaded with bottles containing all kinds of drugs and medicines. I remarked carelessly to Na-a-cha that if he doubted my powers I would gladly burn a hole through his tongue with a drop of fluid from the vial marked "Acid, nitric," but he concluded that my word was sufficient, and after the door was locked to secure us from intrusion he consented to let me open and examine the phylactery and make a sketch of its contents.

To guard against all possible trouble, he put a pinch of *hoddentin* on each of my shoulders, on the crown of my head, and on my chest and back. The same performance was gone through with in his own case. He explained that *hoddentin* was good for men to eat, that it was good medicine for the bear, and that the bear liked to eat it. I thought that herein might be one clew to the reason why the Apache used it as a medicine. The bear loves the *tule* swamp, from which, in days primeval, he sallied out to attack the squaws and children gathering the *tule* powder or *tule* bulb. Poorly armed, as they then were, the Apache must have had great trouble in resisting him; hence they hope to appease him by offering a sacrifice acceptable to his palate.

If acceptable to the chief animal god, as the bear seems to have been, as he certainly was the most dangerous, then it would have been also acceptable to the minor deities like the puma, snake, eagle, etc., and, by an easy transition, to the sun, moon, and other celestial powers. This opinion did not last long, as will be shown. From its constant association with all sacrifices and all acts of worship, *hoddentin* would naturally become itself sanctified and an object of worship, just as rattles, drums, standards, holy grails, etc., in different parts of the world have become fetichistic. I was not in the least surprised when I heard Moses. Henderson reciting a prayer, part of which ran thus:

Hoddentin eshkin, bi hoddentin ashi
(*Hoddentin* child, you *hoddentin* I offer),

and to learn that it was a personification of *hoddentin*.

The fact that the myths of the Apache relate that Assanut-li-je spilled *hoddentin* over the surface of the sky to make the Milky Way may be looked upon as an inchoate form of a calendar, just as the Aztecs transferred to their calendar the reed, rabbit, etc.

So constant is the appearance of *hoddentin* in ceremonies of a religious nature among the Apache that the expression "*hoddentin schlawn*" (plenty of *hoddentin*) has come to mean that a particular performance or place is sacred. Yet, strange to say, this sacred pollen of the *tule* is gathered without any special ceremony; at least, I noticed none when I saw it gathered, although I should not fail to record that at the time of which I speak the Apache and the Apache-Yuma were returning from an arduous campaign, in which blood had been shed, and everything they did—the bathing in the sweat lodges and the singing of the Apache and the plastering of mud upon their heads by the Apache-Yuma—had a reference to the lustration or purgation necessary under such circumstances. Not only men but women may gather the pollen. When the *tule* is not within reach our cat-tail rush is used. Thus, the Chiricahua, confined at Fort Pickens, Florida, gathered the pollen of the cat-tail rush, some of which was given me by one of the women who gathered it. Before making an examination into the meaning to be attached to the use of *hoddentin*, it is well to determine whether or not such a powder or anything analogous to it is to be found among the tribes adjacent.

The "Kunque" of the Zuñi and Others.

The term "*kunque*" as it appears in this chapter is one of convenience only. Each *pueblo*, or rather each set of *pueblos*, has its own name in its own language, as, for example, the people of Laguna and Acoma, who employ it in all their ceremonies as freely as do the Zuñi, call it in their tongue "*hiuawa*." In every *pueblo* which I visited—and I visited them all, from Oraibi of Tusayan, on the extreme west, to Picuris, on the extreme east; from Taos, in the far north, to Isleta del Sur, in Texas—I came upon this *kunque*, and generally in such quantities and so openly exposed and so freely used that I was both astonished and gratified; astonished that after centuries of contact with the Caucasian the natives should still adhere with such tenacity to the ideas of a religion supposed to have been extirpated, and gratified to discover a lever which I could employ in prying into the meaning of other usages and ceremonials.

Behind the main door in the houses at Santa Clara, San Ildefonso, Picuris, Laguna, Acoma, San Felipe, Jemez, and other towns, there is a niche containing a bowl or saucer filled with this sacred meal, of which the good housewife is careful to throw a pinch to the sun at early dawn and to the twilight at eventide. In every ceremony among the Pueblos naturally enough, more particularly among those who have been living farthest from the Mexicans, the lavish scattering of sacred meal is the marked feature of the occasion. At the snake dance of the Tusayan, in 1881, the altars were surrounded with baskets of pottery and with flat plaques of reeds, which were heaped high with *kunque*.

When the procession moved out from under the arcade and began to make the round of the sacred stone the air was white with meal, and in my imagination I could see that it was a procession of Druids circling about a "sacred stone" in Ireland previous to the coming of St. Patrick. When the priests threw the snakes down upon the ground it was within a circle traced with *kunque*, and soon the snakes were covered with the same meal flung upon them by the squaws. There was only one scalp left among the Tusayan in 1881, but there were several among the Zuñi, and one or two each at Acoma and Laguna. In every one of these towns *kunque* was offered to the scalps.

At the feast of the Little God of Fire among the Zuñi, in 1881, my personal notes relate that:

......the moment the head of the procession touched the knoll upon which the *pueblo* is built the mass of people began throwing *kunque* upon the Little God and those with him as well as on the ground in front of, beside, and behind them. This *kunque* was contained in sacred basket-shaped bowls of earthenware. The spectators kept the air fairly misty with clouds of the sacred *kunque*. This procession passed around the boundaries of the *pueblo* of Zuñi, stopping at eight holes in the ground for the purpose of enacting a ceremonial of consecration suggestive of the '*terminalia*' of the Romans. They visited each of the holes, which were 18 inches deep and 12 inches square, with a sandstone slab to serve as a cover. Each hole was filled with *kunque* and sacrificial plumes. . . . . 'Every morning of the year, when the sky is clear, at the rising of Lucero [the morning star], at the crowing of the cock, we throw corn flour [*kunque*] to the sun. I am never without my bag of *kunque*; here it is [drawing it from his belt]. Every Zuñi has one. We offer it to the sun for good rain and good crops.'—Interview with Pedro Pino.

Subsequently Pedro went on to describe in detail a phallic dance and ceremony, in which there was a sort of divination. The young maiden who made the lucky guess was richly rewarded, while her less fortunate companions were presented with a handful of *kunque*, which they kept during the ensuing year. This dance is called "*ky'áklu*," and is independent of the great phallic dance occurring in the month of December. Pedro also stated that until very recently the Zuñi were in the habit of celebrating a fire dance at *Noche Buena* (Christmas). There were four piles of wood gathered for the occasion, and upon each the medicine-men threw *kunque* in profusion. This dance, as Pedro described it, closely resembled one mentioned by Landa in his Cosas de Yucatan. High up on the vertical face of the precipice of Tâaiyalana there is a phallic shrine of the Zuñi to which I climbed with Mr. Frank Cushing. We found that the place had been visited by young brides who were desirous of becoming mothers. The offerings in every case included *kunque*.

In the account given in the National Tribune, Washington, District of Columbia, May 20, 1886, of the mode of life of the Zuñi woman Wehwa while in the national capital, and while engaged in the *kirmes*, we read:

> She also strewed sacred corn meal along on her way to the theatre to bring good luck to her and the other dancers. . . . . She has gone from her comfortable room to pray in the street at daylight every morning, whatever the weather has been. . . . . At such times she strews corn meal all around her until the front-door steps and the sidewalk are much daubed with dough. But this is not the corn meal in common use in the United States, but is sacred meal ground in Zuñi with sacred stones. [4]

So long a time has elapsed since any of the Pueblos have been on the warpath that no man can describe their actual war customs except from the dramatic ceremonial of their dances or from the stories told him by the "old men." The following from an eyewitness will therefore be of interest:

> Before the Pueblos reached the heights they were ordered to scale they halted on the way to receive from their chiefs some medicine from the medicine bags which each of them carried about his person. This they rubbed upon their heart, as they said, to make it big and brave, and they also rubbed it upon other parts of their bodies and upon their rides for the same purpose.—Simpson, *Expedition to the Navajo Country* in Senate Doc.

The constant use of *kunque* by the different Pueblo tribes has been noticed from the first days of European contact. In the relation of Don Antonio de Espejo (1583) we are told that upon the approach of the Spaniards to the town of Zaguato, lying 28 leagues west of Zuñi:

> . . . . a great multitude of Indians came forth to meete them, and among the rest their Caçiques, with so great demonstration of joy and gladnes, that they cast much meale of maiz upon the ground for the horses to tread upon.—Hakluyt, *Voyages*, vol. 3.

I am under the impression that the ruins of this village are those near the ranch of Mr. Thomas V. Keam, at Keam's Canyon, Arizona, called by the Navajo "*Talla-hogandi*," meaning "singing house," in

---

4. *Kunque* has added to the cornmeal the meal of two varieties of corn, blue and yellow, a small quantity of pulverized sea shells, and some sand, and when possible a fragment of the blue stone called "*chalchihuitl*." In grinding the meal on the *metates* the squaws are stimulated by the medicine-men who keep up a constant singing and drumming.

reference to the Spanish mission which formerly existed there. This village is, as I have hitherto shown, the ruin of the early *pueblo* of Awáatubi.

It is gratifying to observe that the Spanish writer in the remote wilds of America struck upon an important fact in ethnology: that the throwing of "*harina*" or flour by the people of Tusayan (Mohoçe or Moqui), Cibola, and Zuñi (observe the odd separation of "Zibola" from either Moqui or Zuñi) was identical with the "*carnestolendas*" of Spain, in which, on Shrove Tuesday, the women and girls cover all the men they meet with flour. The men are not at all backward in returning the compliment, and the streets are at times filled with the farinaceous dust.

"*Harina de maiz azul*" is used by Mexicans in their religious ceremonies, especially those connected with the water deities, the Peruvians, when they bathed and sacrificed to cure themselves of sickness. The *kunque* of the Peruvians very closely resembled that of the Zuñi. We read that it was a compound of different-coloured maize ground up with sea shells. The Peruvians had a Priapic idol called Hua-canqui.

The tribes seen on the Rio Colorado in 1540 by Alarcon:

. . . . carry also certaine little long bagges about an hand broade tyed to their left arme, which serve them also instead of brasers for their bowes, full of the powder of a certaine herbe, whereof they make a certaine beverage—(Hakluyt *Voyages.*)

We are at a loss to know what this powder was, unless *hoddentin.* The Indians came down to receive the son of the sun, as Alarcon led them to believe him to be, in full gala attire, and no doubt neglected nothing that would add to their safety.

Kohl speaks of seeing inside the medicine *wigwam*, during the great medicine ceremonies of the Ojibwa, "a snow-white powder." In an address delivered by Dr. W. J. Hoffman before the Anthropological Society of Washington, D. C., May 3, 1888, upon the symbolism of the Midé, Jes'sakkid, and Wâbeno of the Ojibwa of Minnesota, he stated in reply to a question from me that he had not been able to find any of the "snow-white powder" alluded to by Kohl in Kitchi-gami.

In Yucatan, when children were baptized, one of the ceremonies was that the *chac*, or priest in charge, should give the youngster a pinch of corn meal, which the boy threw in the fire. These *chacs* were priests of the god who presided over baptism and over hunting.

When Capt. John Smith was captured by the Pamunkey tribe of Virginia in 1607 he was taken to "a long house," where, on the morning following "a great grim fellow" came skipping in, "all painted over with coale, mingled with oyle. With most strange gestures and passions he began his invocation, and environed the fire with a circle of meale." This priest was followed by six others, who "with their rattles began a song, which ended, the chiefe priest layd downe five wheat cornes." This ceremony was apparently continued during the day and repeated on the following two days. Capt. Smith's reception by the medicine-men of the Virginians is described by Picart. These medicine-men are called "*prêtres*," and we are informed that they sang "*des chants magiques*." The grains of wheat (*grains de blé*) were "*rangez cinq à cinq*."

While the Baron de Graffenreid was a prisoner in the hands of the Tuscarora, on the Neuse River, in 1711, the conjurer or high priest ("the priests are generally magicians and even conjure up the devil") "made two white rounds, whether of flour or white sand, I do not know, just in front of us."—*Colonial Records of North Carolina*, 1886, vol. 1.

Lafitau says of one of the medicine women of America: "*Elle commença d'abord par préparer un espace de terrain qu'elle nétoya bien & qu'elle couvrit de farine, ou de cendre tres-bien bluttée (je ne me souviens pas exactement laquelle des deux).*" (She began by preparing an area of land, she cleaned it well, and that she covered well with flour or ash (I do not remember exactly which of the two).

In a description of the ceremonial connected with the first appearance of the *catamenia* in a Navajo squaw, there is no reference to a use of anything like *hoddentin*, unless it may be the corn which was ground into meal for a grand feast, presided over by a medicine-man. When a woman is grinding corn or cooking, and frequently when any of the Navajo, male or female, are eating, a handful of corn meal is put in the fire as an offering (to the sun).—Personal notes of May 26. 1881; conversation with Chi and Damon at Fort Defiance. Navajo Agency, Arizona.

Maj. Backus, U. S. Army, describes certain ceremonies which he saw performed by the Navajo at a sacred spring near Fort Defiance, Arizona, which seems to have once been a geyser:

I once visited it with three other persons and an Indian doctor, who carried with him live small bags, each containing some vegetable or mineral substance, all differing in colour. At the spring each bag was opened and a small quantity of its contents was put into the right hand of each person present. Each visitor in succession, was then required to kneel down by the spring side, to place his closed hand in the water up to his elbow, and after a brief interval to open his hand and let fall its contents into the spring. The hand was then slowly withdrawn and each one was then permitted to drink and retire.—Maj. Backus.

He showed me, as a special favour, that which give him his power a bag with some reddish powder in it. He allowed me to handle it and smell this mysterious stuff, and pointed out two little dolls or images, which, he said, gave him authority over the souls of others; it was for their support that flour and water were placed in small birch-rind saucers in front.—The medicine-men of the Swampy Crees, as described in Bishop of Rupert's Land's works, quoted by Henry Youle Hind, *Canadian Exploring Expedition*, vol.1.

In the narrative of the Jeannette Arctic expedition, Dr. Newcomb says:

One day, soon after New Year's, I was out walking with one of the Indians. Noticing the new moon, he stopped, faced it, and, blowing out his breath, he spoke to it, invoking success in hunting. The moon, he said, was '*Tyunne*,' or ruler of deers, bears, seals, and walrus.

The ceremony herein described I have no doubt was analogous in every respect to *hoddentin*-throwing. As the Indians mentioned were undoubtedly Tinueh, my surmise seems all the more reasonable.—Personal notes, November 22. 1885, at Baker's ranch, summit of the Sierra Ancha, Arizona.

Tanner relates that among the Ojibwa the two best hunters of the band had "each a little leather sack of medicine, consisting of certain roots pounded line and mixed with red paint, to be applied to the little images or figures of the animals we wish to kill."

Attached to the necklace of human fingers before described, captured from one of the chief medicine-men of the Cheyenne Indians, is a bag containing a powder very closely resembling *hoddentin*, if not *hoddentin* itself.

It is said that the Asinai made sacrifice to the scalps of their enemies, as did the Zuñi as late as 1881.

Perrot says the Indians of Canada had large medicine bags, which he calls "*pindikossan,*" which, among other things, contained "*des racines ou des poudres pour leur servir de médecines,*" (roots or powders for use of medicines).

In an article on the myth of Manibozho, by Squier, in *American Historical Magazine Review,* 1848, may be found an account of the adventures of two young heroes, one of whom is transferred to the list of gods. He commissioned his comrade to bring him offerings of a white wolf, a polecat, some pounded maize, and eagles' tails.

Cameron met an old chief on the shores of Lake Tanganyika, of whom he says: "His forehead and hair were daubed with vermilion, yellow, and white powder, the pollen of flowers."

The voodoo ceremonies of the negroes of New Orleans, which would seem to have been transplanted from Africa, include a sprinkling of the congregation with a meal which has been blessed by the head medicine-man or conjurer.

The use of these sacred powders during so many different religious festivals and ceremonies would seem to resemble closely that made by the Apache of *hoddentin* and the employment of *kunque* by the Zuñi and others; and from Asia it would seem that practices very similar in character found their way into Europe.

The Zuñi, in preparing *kunque* or sacred meal for their religions festivals, invariably made it in the form of a pyramid resting upon one of their flat baskets.

Mr. Frank H. Cushing informs me that there is an annual feast among the Zuñi in which are to be seen cakes answering essentially to the preceding description.

Hoddentin a Prehistoric Food.

The peculiar manner in which the medicine-men of the Apache use the *hoddentin* (that is, by putting a pinch upon their own tongues); the fact that men and women make use of it in the same way, as a restorative when exhausted; its appearance in myth in connection with Assanutlije, the goddess who supplied the Apache and Navajo with so many material benefits, all combine to awaken the suspicion that in *hoddentin* we have stumbled upon a prehistoric food now reserved for sacrificial purposes only. That the underlying idea of sacrifice is a food offered to some god is a proposition in which Herbert Spencer and W. Robertson Smith concur.

In my opinion, this definition is incomplete; a perfect sacrifice is that in which a *prehistoric* food is offered to a god, and, although in the family oblations of everyday life we meet with the food of the present generation, it would not be difficult to show that where the whole community unites in a function of exceptional importance the propitiation of the deities will be effected by foods whose use has long since faded away from the memory of the laity.

The sacred feast of stewed puppy and wild turnips forms a prominent part of the sun dance of the Sioux, and had its parallel in a collation of boiled puppy (*catullus*), of which the highest civic and ecclesiastical dignitaries of pagan Rome partook at stated intervals.

The reversion of the Apache to the food of his ancestors—the *hoddentin*—as a religious offering has its analogue in the unleavened bread and other obsolete farinaceous products which the ceremonial of more enlightened races has preserved from oblivion. Careful consideration of the narrative of Cabeza de Vaca sustains this conclusion. In the western portion of his wanderings we learn that for from thirty to forty days he and his comrades passed through tribes which for one-third of the year had to live on "the powder of straw" (on the powder of *bledos*), and that afterwards the Spaniards came among people who raised corn. At that time, Vaca, whether we believe that he ascended the Rio Concho or kept on up the Rio Grande, was in a region where he would certainly have encountered the ancestors of our Apache tribe and their brothers the Navajo.

This powder (*polvo*) of *paja* or grass might at first sight seem to be grass seeds; but why not say "flour," as on other occasions? The phrase is an obscure one, but not more obscure than the description of the whole journey. In the earlier writings of the Spaniards there is ambiguity because the new arrivals endeavoured to apply the names of their own plants and animals to all that they saw in the western continent. Neither Castañeda nor Cabeza de Vaca makes mention of *hoddentin*, but Vaca does say that when he had almost ended his journey: "*La côte ne possède pas de maïs; on n'y mange que de la poudre de paille de blette,*" (the coast does not have corn; we do not eat the powder straw chard.) "*Blette*" is the same as the Spanish "*bledos.*"

> *Nous parvînmes chez une peuplade qui, pendant le tiers de l'année, ne vit que de poudre de paille.* We met with a people, who the third part of the yeere eate no other thing save the powder of straw.—Relation of Cabeza de Vaca. in *Purchas*, vol. 4.

Davis, who seems to have followed Herrera, says:

These Indians lived one-third of the year on the powder of a certain straw . . . . After leaving this people they again arrived in a country of permanent habitations, where they found an abundance of maize. The inhabitants gave them maize both in grain and flour.

The Tusayan Indians were formerly in the habit of adding a trifle of chopped straw to their bread, but more as our own bakers would use bran than as a regular article of diet.

Barcia makes no allusion to anything resembling *hoddentin* or "*polvos de bledos*" in his brief account of Vaca's journey. But Buckingham Smith, in his excellent translation of Vaca's narrative, renders "*polvos de paja*" thus:

It was probably the seed of grass which they ate. I am told by a distinguished explorer that the Indians to the west collect it of different kinds and from the powder make bread, some of which is quite palatable.

And for "*polvos de bledos*":

The only explanation I can offer for these words is little satisfactory. It was the practice of the Indians of both New Spain and New Mexico to beat the ear of young maize, while in the milk, to a thin paste, hang it in festoons in the sun, and, being thus dried, was preserved for winter use.

This explanation is very unsatisfactory. Would not Vaca have known it was corn and have said so? On the contrary, he remarks in that very line in Smith's own translation: "There is no maize on the coast."

The appearance of all kinds of grass seeds in the food of nearly all the aborigines of our south-western territory is a fact well known, but what is to be demonstrated is the extensive use of the "powder" of the *tule* or cat-tail rush. Down to our day, the Apache have used not only the seeds of various grasses, but the bulb of the wild hyacinth and the bulb of the *tule*. The former can be eaten either raw or cooked, but the *tule* bulb is always roasted between hot stones. The taste of the hyacinth bulb is somewhat like that of raw chestnuts. That of the roasted *tule* bulb is sweet and not at all disagreeable.

Father Jacob Baegert enumerates among the foods of the Indians of southern California "the roots of the common reed" (*i. e.,* of the *tule*).

Father Alegre, speaking of the tribes living near the Lagnna San

Pedro, in latitude 28° north—two hundred leagues north of the City of Mexico—says that they make their bread of the root, which is very frequent in their lakes, and which is like the plant called the "*anea*" or rush in Spain.

The Indians of the Atlantic Slope made bread of the bulb of a plant which Capt. John Smith says "grew like a flag in marshes." It was roasted and made into loaves called "*tuckahoe*."

Kalm, in his *Travels in North America*, says of the *tuckahoe*:

> It grows in several swamps and marshes mid is commonly plentiful. The hogs greedily dig up its roots with their noses in such places, and the Indians of Carolina likewise gather it in their rambles in the woods, dry it in the sun, grind, and make bread of it. Whilst the root is fresh it is harsh and acrid, but, being dried, it loses the greater part of its acrimony. To judge by these qualities, the *tuckahoe* may very likely be the Arum *virginianum*.

The Shoshoni and Bannock of Idaho and Montana eat the *tule* bulb. "

Something analogous to *hoddentin* is mentioned by the chronicler of Drake's voyage along the California coast about A. D. 1540. Speaking of the decorations of the chiefs of the Indians seen near where San Francisco now stands, he says another mark of distinction was:

> . . . . . a certain downe, which groweth up in the countrey upon an herbe much like our lectuce, which exceeds any other downe in the world for finenesse and beeing layed upon their cawles, by no winds can be removed. Of such estimation is this herbe amongst them that the downe thereof is not lawfull to be worne, but of such persons as are about the king, ... and the seeds are not used but onely in sacrifice to their gods.

Mr. Cushing informs me that *hoddentin* is mentioned as a food in the myths of the Zuñi under the name of *oneya*, from *oellu*, "food."

"Bledos" of Ancient Writers Its Meaning.

Lafltan gives a description of the Iroquois mode of preparing for the warpath. He says that the Iroquois and Huron called war "*n'ondoutagette*" and "*gaskenragette*." "*Le terme Ondouta signifie le duvet qu'on tire de l'épy des Roseaux de Marais & signifie aussi la plante toute entiere, dont ils se servent pour faire les nattes sur qnoi ils couchent, de sorte qu'il y a apparence qu'ils avoient affecté ce terme pour la Guerre, parce que chaque Guerrier portoit avec soy sa natte dans ces sortes d'expeditions.*" This does not seem to be the correct explanation. Rather, it was because they undoubtedly made some sacrificial meal of this *"duvet,"* or pollen, and used it as much as the Apache do *hoddentin,* their sacred meal made of the pollen of the *tule,* which is surely a species of *"roseaux de marais."*

Castañeda speaks of the people beyond Chichilticale making a bread of the *mesquite* which kept good for a whole year. He seems to have been well informed regarding the vegetable foods of the tribes passed through by Coronado's expedition.

That the *"blettes"* or "bledos" did not mean the same as grass is a certainty after we have examined the old writers, who each and all show that the *bledos* meant, a definite kind of plant, although exactly what this plant was they fail to inform us. It cannot be intended for the sunflower, which is mentioned distinctly by a number of writers as an article of diet among the Indians of the Southwest.

TZOALLI.

In the month called Tepeilhuitl the Aztecs made snakes of twigs and covered them with dough of *bledos* (a kind of grain or hay seed). Upon these they placed figures, representing mountains, but shaped like young children.' This month was the thirteenth on the Mexican calendar, which began on our February 1. This would put it October 1, or thereabout.

Squier cites Torquemada's description of the sacrifices called Eca-totontin, offered to the mountains by the Mexicans. In these they made figures of serpents and children and covered them with "dough," named by them *tzoalli,* composed of the seeds of *bledos.*

A dramatic representation strongly resembling those described in the two preceding paragraphs was noted among the Tusayan of Arizona by Mr. Taylor, a missionary, in 1881, and has been mentioned at length in The Snake Dance of the Moquis. Clavigero relates that the Mexican priests "all eat a certain kind of gruel which they call *Etzalli."*

The ceremonial manner in which these seeds were ground recalls the fact that the Zuñi regard the stones used for grinding *kunque* as sacred and will not employ them for any other purpose.

Blessed blankets are to be seen at the Zuñi feast of the Little God of Fire, which occurs in the month of December. It is a curious thing that the blessed blankets of the Zuñi are decorated with the butterfly, which appeared upon the royal robes of Montezuma.

What other seeds were used in the fabrication of these idols is not very essential to our purpose, but it may be pointed out that one of them was the seed of the "*agenjo*," which was the "*chenopodium* "or "*artemisia*," known to us as the "sagebrush."

Gomara's statement, that while these cakes of maize and worm-wood seed were cooking the young men were beating on drums, would find its parallel in any account that might be written of the behaviour of the Zuñi, while preparing for their sacred feasts. The squaws grind the meal to be used on these occasions to the accompaniment of singing by the medicine-men and much drumming by a baud of assistants selected from among the young men and boys.

Mr. Francis La Flèche, a nearly full-blood Omaha Indian, read before the Anthropological Society of Washington, B.C., in 1888, a paper descriptive of the funeral customs of his people, in which he related that when an Indian was supposed to be threatened with death the medicine-men would go in a lodge sweat-bath with him and sing, and at the same time "pronouncing certain incantations and sprinkling the body of the client with the powder of the *artemisia*, supposed to be the food of the ghosts."—From the account of lecture appearing in the *Evening Star*, Washington, D. C., May 19 1888.

To say that a certain powder is the food of the ghosts of a tribe is to say indirectly that the same powder was once the food of the tribe's ancestors.

GENERAL USE OF THE POWDER AMONG INDIANS.

This very general dissemination among the Indians of the American continent of the sacred use of the powder of the *tule*, of images, idols, or sacrificial cakes made of such prehistoric foods, certainly suggests that the Apache and the Aztecs, among whom they seem to have been most freely used on ceremonial occasions, were invaders in the country they respectively occupied, comparatively recent in their arrival among the contiguous tribes like the Zuñi and Tusayan who on corresponding occasions offered to their gods a cultivated food like corn. The Tlascaltec were known in Mexico as the "bread people," possibly because they had been acquainted with the cultivation of the cereals long before the Aztecs. Similarly, there was a differentiation of the Apache from the sedentary Pueblos.

The Apache were known to all the villages of the Pueblos as a "corn-buying tribe," as will presently be shown. It is true that in isolated cases and in widely separated sections the Apache have for nearly two centuries been a corn-planting people, because we find accounts in the Spanish chronicles of the discovery and destruction by their military expeditions of "*trojes*" or magazines of Apache corn near the San Francisco (or Verde) River, in the present Territory of Arizona, as early as the middle of the last century. But the general practice of the tribe was to purchase its bread or meal from the Pueblos at such times as hostilities were not an obstacle to free trade.

There was this difference to be noted between the Apache and the Aztecs: The latter had been long enough in the valley of Anahuac to learn and adopt many new foods, as we learn from Duran, who relates that at their festivals in honour of Tezcatlipoca, or those made in pursuance of some vow, the woman cooked an astonishing variety of bread, just as, at the festivals of the Zuñi, Tusayan, and other Pueblos in our own time, thirty different kinds of preparations of corn may be found. I was personally informed by old Indians in the pueblos along the Bio Grande that they had been in the habit of trading with the Apache and Comanche of the Staked Plains of Texas until within very recent years; in fact, I remember seeing such a party of Pueblos on its return from Texas in 1869, as it reached Fort Craig, New Mexico, where I was then stationed. I bought a buffalo robe from them.

The principal article of sale on the side of the Pueblos was cornmeal. The Zuñi also carried on this mixed trade and hunting, as I was informed by the old chief Pedro Pino and others. The Tusayan denied that they had ever traded with the Apache so far to the east as the buffalo country, but asserted that the Comanche had once sent a large body of their people over to Walpi to trade with the Tusayan, among whom they remained for two years. There was one buffalo robe among the Tusayan at their snake dance in 1881, possibly obtained from the Ute to the north of them.

The trade carried on by the "buffalo" Indians with the Pueblos was noticed by Don Juan de Onate as early as 1599. He describes them as "dressed in skins, which they also carried into the settled provinces to sell, and brought back in return cornmeal."

Gregg speaks of the "Comancheros" or Mexicans and Pueblos who ventured out on the plains to trade with the Comanche, the principal article of traffic being bread. Whipple refers to this trade as carried on with all the nomadic tribes of the Llano Estacado, one of which we know to have been the eastern division of the Apache. The principal article bartered with the wild tribes was flour, *i. e.*, cornmeal.

In another place he tells us of "Pueblo Indians from Santo Domingo, with flour and bread to barter with the Kái-ò-wàs and Comanches for buffalo robes and horses." Again, Mexicans were seen with flour, bread, and tobacco, "bound for Comanche land to trade. We had no previous idea of the extent of this Indian trade." Only one other reference to this intertribal commerce will be introduced.

Vetancurt mentions that the Franciscan friars, between 1630 and 1680, had erected a magnificent "temple" to "Our Lady of the Angels of Porciuncula," and that the walls were so thick that offices were established in their concavities. On each side of this temple, which was erected in the *pueblo* of Pecos (situated at or near the head of the Pecos River, about 30 miles southeast of Santa Fe, New Mexico, on the eastern rim of the Llano Estacado), were three towers.

At the foot of the hill was a plain about one league in circumference, to which the Apache resorted for trade. These were the Apache living on the plains of Texas. They brought with them buffalo robes, deer skins and other things to exchange for corn. They came with their dog-trains loaded, and there were more than five hundred traders arriving each year.

Observe that here we have the first and only reference to the use of dog trains by the Apache who in every other case make their women carry all plunder in baskets on their backs.

In this same extract from Vetancurt there is a valuable remark about Quivira: "*Este es el paso para los reinos de la Quivira,*" (this is the step to the kingdoms of Quivira).

ANALOGUES OF HODDENTIN.

No allusion has yet been made to the *hoddentin* of the Navajo, who are the brothers of the Apache. Surgeon Matthews has referred to it under the name of *tqa-di-tin*, or *ta-di-tin*, "the pollen, especially the pollen of corn."

This appears to me to be a very interesting case of a compromise between the religious ideas of two entirely different systems or sects. The Navajo, as now known to us, are the offspring of the original Apache or Tinneh invaders and the refugees from the Rio Grande and Zuñ Pueblos, who fled to the fierce and cruel Apache to seek safety from the fiercer and more cruel Spanish.

The Apache, we have shown, offer up in sacrifice their traditional food, the pollen of the *tule*. The Zuñi, as we have also shown, offer up their traditional food, the meal of corn, to which there have since been added sea shells and other components with a symbolical significance. The Navajo, the progeny of both, naturally seek to effect a combination or compromise of the two systems and make use of the pollen of the corn. Kohl narrates an Ojibwa legend to the effect that their god Menaboju, returning from the warpath, painted his face with "pleasant yellow stripes . . . of the yellow foam that covers the water in spring," and he adds that this is "probably the yellow pollen that falls from the pine." He quotes another legend of the magic, red powder for curing diseases once given by the snake spirit of the waters to an Ojibwa.

In writing the description of the Snake Dance of the Moquis of Arizona, I ventured to advance the surmise that the corn flour with which the sacred snakes were covered, and with which the air was whitened, would be found upon investigation to be closely related to the crithomancy or divination by grains of the cereals, as practiced among the ancient Greeks. Crithomancy, strictly speaking, meant a divination by grains of corn. The expression which I should have employed was alphitomancy, a divination "by meal, flower, or branne." But both methods of divination have been noticed among the aborigines of America.

Father Breboeuf relates that at the Huron feast of the dead, which occurred every 8 or 10 years and which he saw at Ossossane, "a few grains of Indian corn were thrown by the women upon the sacred relics."

THE DOWN OF BIRDS IN CEREMONIAL OBSERVANCES.

No exhaustive and accurate examination of the subject of *hoddentin* could be made without bringing the investigator face to face with the curious analogue of "down" throwing and sprinkling which seemingly obtains with tribes which at some period of their history have been compelled to rely upon birds as a main component of their diet.

Examples of this are to be met with on both sides of the Pacific as well as in remote Australia, and were the matter more fully examined there is no doubt that some other identifications might be made in very unexpected quarters. The down used by the Tchuktchi on occasions of ceremony had a suggestion of religion about it.

> On leaving the shore, they sung and danced. One who stood at the head of the boat was employed in plucking out the feathers of a bird's skin and blowing them in the air.

In Langsdorff's *Travels* we learn that some of the dancers of the

Koluschan of Sitka have their heads powdered with the small down feathers of the white-headed eagle and ornamented with ermine; also, that the hair and bodies of the Indians at the mission of Saint Joseph, New California, were powdered with down feathers."

The Indians from the North Pacific coast seen visiting the mission of San Francisco, by Kotzebue in 1816, "had their long disordered hair covered with down."

Bancroft says of the Nootka of the northwest coast of British America: "the hair is powdered plentifully with white feathers, which are regarded as the crowning ornament for manly dignity in all these regions."

The bird's down used by the Haida of British North America in their dances seems very closely related to *hoddentin*. They not only put it upon their own persons, but "delight to communicate it to their partners in bowing," and also "blow it into the air at regular intervals through a painted tube." They also scattered down as a sign of welcome to the first European navigators.

In all these dances, ceremonial visits, and receptions of strangers the religious element can be discerned more or less plainly. The Indians west of the Mississippi with whom Father Hennepin was a prisoner in 1680, and who appear to have been a branch of the Sioux (Issati or Santee and Nadouessan), had a grand dance to signalize the killing of a bear. On this occasion, it was participated in by the "*principaux chefs et guerriers.*"

"Swan's and bustard's down" was used by the Accancess [*i. e.,* the Arkansas of the Siouan stock] in their religious ceremonies.

Of the war dress of the members of the Five Nations we learn from an early writer:

Their heads [previously denuded of all hair except that of the crown] are painted red down to the eyebrows and sprinkled over with white down.—Maj. Rogers, Account of North America, in Knox's *Voyages,* vol. 2.

The Indians of Virginia at their war dances painted themselves to make them more terrible: "*Pour se rendre plus terriblee, ils sement des plumes, du duvet, ou du poil de quelque bete sur la peinture toute fraiche.*" (They spread feathers, down or the hair of animals on the fresh paint). Down was also used by the medicine-men of the Carib.

Speaking of the "duvet" or down, with which many American savage tribes deck themselves, Picart observes very justly: "*Cet ornementest bizarre, mais dans le fond 1'est il beaucoup plus que cette poudre d'or dont les Anciens, se poudroient la tête, ou que cette poudre composée d'amidon avec laquelle nos petits maitres modernes affectent de blanchir leurs cheveux ou leurs perruques!*" (This ornament is bizarre but in reality is it much more than the gold dust which the elders powdered their head or the powder made of starch that modern masters bleach their hair or wigs?)

Picart does not say, and perhaps it would not be wise for us to surmise, that these modes of powdering had a religious origin.

The use of ashes also occurs among the Zuñi, the Apache (at times). Ashes are also "thrown in the way of a whirlwind to appease it."

The French writers mention among the ceremonies of the Natchez one in which the Great Sun "gathered dust, which he threw back over his head, and turned successively to the four quarters of the world in repeating the same act of throwing dust."

Clay-Eating.

The Muiscas had in their language the word "*jipetera*," a "disease from eating dirt." Whether the word "dirt" as here employed means filth, or earth and clay, is not plain; it probably means clay and earth.

Venegas asserts that the Indians of California ate earth. The traditions of the Indians of San Juan Capistrano, California, and vicinity show that "they had fed upon a kind of clay," which they "often used upon their heads by way of ornament."

The Tátu Indians of California mix "red earth into their acorn bread . . . to make the bread sweet and make it go further."

Long relates that when the young warrior of the Oto or Omaha tribes goes out on his first fast he "rubs his person over with a whitish clay," but he does not state that he ate it.

Sir John Franklin relates that the banks of the Mackenzie River in British North America contain layers of a kind of unctuous mud, probably similar to that found near the Orinoco, which the Tinneh Indians "use occasionally as food during seasons of famine, and even at other times chew as an amusement. . . . It has a milky taste and the flavour is not disagreeable."

Father de Smet says of the Athapascan:

Many wandering families of the Carrier tribe . . . have their teeth worn to the gums by the earth and sand they swallow with their nourishment.

This does not seem to have been intentionally eaten.

The Apache and Navajo branches of the Athapascan family are not unacquainted with the use of clay as a comestible, although among the former it is now scarcely ever used and among the latter used only as a condiment to relieve the bitterness of the taste of the wild potato; in the same manner it is known to both the Zuñi and Tusayan.

Wallace says that eating dirt was "a very common and destructive habit among Indians and half-breeds in the houses of the whites.

The earth which is eaten by the Ottomacs [of the Rio Orinoco] is fat and unctuous.

Waitz cites Heusinger as saying that the Ottomacs of the Rio Orinoco eat large quantities of a fatty clay.

Prehistoric Foods Used in Covenants.

It has been shown that the Apache, on several occasions, as when going out to meet strangers, entering into solemn agreements, etc., made use of the *hoddentin*. A similar use of food, generally prehistoric, can be noted in other regions of the world.

Sacred breads and cakes

Practices analogous to those referred to are to be noted among the Pueblo Indians. They offer not only the *kunque*, but bread also in their sacrifices.

In the sacred rabbit hunt of the Zuñi, which occurs four times a year and is carried on for the purpose of procuring meat for the sacred eagles confined in cages, a great fire was made on the crest of a hill, into which were thrown piles of bread crusts and in the smoke of which the boomerangs or rabbit sticks were held while the hunter recited in an audible tone and with downcast head the prayers prescribed for the occasion. One of the early Spanish writers informs us that the women of the *pueblo* of Santo Domingo, on the Rio Grande, offered bread on bended knees to their idols and then preserved it for the remainder of the year, and the house which did not have a supply of such blessed bread was regarded as unfortunate and exposed to danger.

Galena.

At times one may find in the "medicine" of the more prominent and influential of the chiefs and medicine-men of the Apache little sacks which, when opened, are found to contain pounded galena; this they tell me is a "great medicine," fully equal to *hoddentin*, but more difficult to obtain. It is used precisely as *hoddentin* is used; that is, both as a face paint and as a powder to be thrown to the sun or other elements to be propitiated. The Apache are reluctant to part with it, and from living Apache I have never obtained more than one small sack of it.

No one seems to understand the reason for its employment. Mr. William M. Beebe has suggested that perhaps the fact that galena always crystallizes in cubes, and that it would thus seem to have a mysterious connection with the cardinal points to which all nomadic peoples pay great attention as being invested with the power of keeping wanderers from going astray, would not be without influence upon the minds of the medicine-men, who are quick to detect and to profit by all false analogies. The conjecture appears to me to be a most plausible one, but I can submit it only as a conjecture, for no explanation of the kind was received from any of the Indians. All that I can say is that whenever procurable it was always used by the Apache on occasions of unusual importance and solemnity and presented as a round disk painted in the centre of the forehead.

The significance of all these markings of the face among savage and half-civilized nations is a subject deserving of the most careful research; like the sectarial marks of the Hindus, all, or nearly all, the marks made upon the faces of American Indians have a meaning beyond the ornamental or the grotesque.

Galena was observed in use among the tribes seen by Cabeza de Vaca. The *Encyclopaedia Britannica* says that the Peruvians used it for "amulets;" so also did the Apache. What Vaca took for antimony was pounded galena no doubt. He was by this time in or near the Rocky Mountains.

On the northwest coast of America we read of the natives:

One, however, as he came near, took out from his bosom some iron or lead-coloured micaceous earth and drew marks with it across his cheeks in the shape of two pears, stuffed his nostrils with grass, and thrust thin pieces of bone through the cartilage of his nose.—William Coxe *Russian Discoveries Between Asia and America.*

It is more than probable that some of the face-painting with "black earth," "ground charcoal," etc., to which reference is made by the early writers, may have been galena, which substance makes a deep-black mark. The natives would be likely to make use of their most sacred powder upon first meeting with mysterious strangers like Vaca and his companions. So, when the expedition of La Salle reached the mouth of the Ohio, in 1680, the Indians are described as fasting and making superstitious sacrifices; among other things, they marked themselves with "black earth" and with "ground charcoal."

Corbusier says of the Apache-Yuma: "Galena and burnt *mescal* are used on their faces, the former to denote auger or as war paint, being spread all over the face, except the chin and nose, which are painted red."

Occasionally with the bones of the dead are noticed small cubes of galena; and in our collection is a ball of this ore, weighing a pound and two ounces, which was taken from a mound, and which probably did service, enveloped in raw hide, as some form of weapon. Galena was much prized by the former inhabitants of North America. "The frequent occurrence of galena on the altars of the sacrificial mounds proves, at any rate, that the ancient inhabitants attributed a peculiar value to it, deeming it worthy to be offered as a sacrificial gift."

The Izze-Kloth or Medicine Cord of the Apache

There is probably no more mysterious or interesting portion of the religious or "medicinal" equipment of the Apache Indian, whether he be medicine-man or simply a member of the laity, than the "*izze-kloth*" or medicine cord, illustrations of which accompany this text. Less, perhaps, is known concerning it than any other article upon which he relies in his distress.

I regret very much to say that I am unable to afford the slightest clew to the meaning of any of the parts or appendages of the cords which I have seen or which I have procured. Some excuse for this is to be found in the fact that the Apache look upon these cords as so sacred that strangers are not allowed to see them, much less handle them or talk about them. I made particular effort to cultivate the most friendly and, when possible, intimate relations with such of the Apache and other medicine-men as seemed to offer the best chance for obtaining information in regard to this and other matters, but I am compelled to say with no success at all.

I did advance so far in my schemes that Na-a-cha, a prominent medicine-man of the Tonto Apache, promised to let me have his cord, but as an eruption of hostility on the part of the tribe called me away from the San Carlos Agency, the opportunity was lost. Ramon, one of the principal medicine-men of the Chiricahua Apache, made me the same promise concerning the cord which he wore and which figures in these plates. It was, unfortunately, sent me by mail, and, although the best in the series and really one of the best I have ever been fortunate enough to see on either living or dead, it was not accompanied by a description of the symbolism of the different articles attached. Ramon also gave me the head-dress which he wore in the spirit or

FIG. 1. SINGLE-STRAND MEDICINE CORD (ZUÑI).

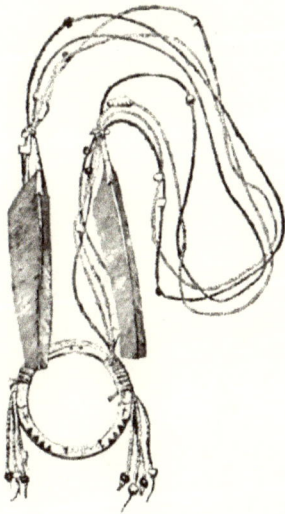

FIG. 2. FOUR-STRAND MEDICINE CORD (APACHE).

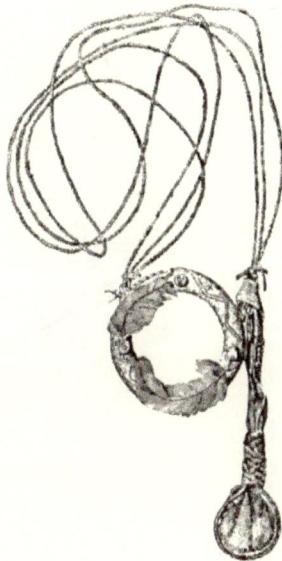

FIG. 3. THREE-STRAND MEDICINE CORD (APACHE).

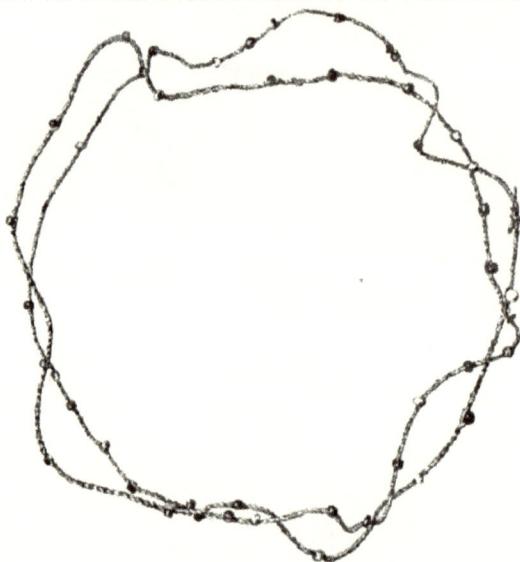

FIG. 4. TWO-STRAND MEDICINE CORD (APACHE)

FIG. 5. FOUR-STRAND MEDICINE CORD (APACHE)

ghost dance, and explained everything thereon, and I am satisfied that he would also, while in the same frame of mind, have given me all the information in his power in regard to the sacred or medicine cord as well, had I been near him.

There are some things belonging to these cords which I understand from having had them explained at other times, but there are others about which I am in extreme doubt and ignorance. There are four specimens of medicine cords represented and it is worthwhile to observe that they were used as one, two, three, and four strand cords, but whether this fact means that they belonged to medicine-men or to warriors of different degrees I did not learn nor do I venture to conjecture.

The single-strand medicine cord with the thirteen olivella shells belonged to a Zuñi chief, one of the priests of the sacred order of the bow, upon whose wrist it was worn as a sign of his exalted rank in the tribe. I obtained it as a proof of his sincerest friendship and with injunctions to say nothing about it to his own people, but no explanation was made at the moment of the signification of the wristlet or cord itself or of the reason for using the olivella shells of that particular number or for placing them as they were placed.

One of the four-strand cords was obtained from Ramon and is the most beautiful and the most valuable of the lot. Ramon called my attention to the important fact that it was composed of four strands and that originally each had been stained a different colour. These colours were probably yellow, blue, white, and black, although the only ones still discernible at this time are the yellow and the blue.

The three-strand cord was sent to me at Washington by my old friend, Al. Seiber, a scout who has been living among the Apache for twenty-five years. No explanation accompanied it and it was probably procured from the body of some dead warrior during one of the innumerable scouts and skirmishes which Seiber has had with this warlike race during his long term of service against them. The two strand cord was obtained by myself so long ago that the circumstances connected with it have escaped my memory.

These cords, in their perfection, are decorated with beads and shells strung along at intervals, with pieces of the sacred green *chalchihuitl*, which has had such a mysterious ascendancy over the minds of the American Indians—Aztec, Peruvian, Quiche, as well as the more savage tribes, like the Apache and Navajo; with petrified wood, rock crystal, eagle down, claws of the hawk or eaglet, claws of the bear, rattle of the rattlesnake, buckskin bags of *hoddentin*, circles of buckskin in which are inclosed pieces of twigs and branches of trees which have been struck by lightning, small fragments of the abalone shell from the Pacific coast, and much other sacred paraphernalia of a similar kind.

That the use of these cords was reserved for the most sacred and important occasions, I soon learned; they were not to be seen on occasions of no moment, but the dances for war, medicine, and summoning the spirits at once brought them out, and every medicine-man of any consequence would appear with one hanging from his right shoulder over his left hip. Only the chief medicine-men can make them, and after being made and before being assumed by the new owner they must be sprinkled Ramon told me, with "*heap hoddentin*," a term meaning that there is a great deal of attendant ceremony of a religious character.

These cords will protect a man while on the warpath, and many of the Apache believe firmly that a bullet will have no effect upon the warrior wearing one of them. This is not their only virtue by any means; the wearer can tell who has stolen ponies or other property from him or from his friends, can help the crops, and cure the sick. If the circle attached to one of these cords (see Fig. 2) is placed upon the head it will at once relieve any ache, while the cross attached to another (see Fig. 5) prevents the wearer from going astray, no matter where he may be; in other words, it has some connection with cross-trails and the four cardinal points to which the Apache pay the strictest attention. The Apache assured me that these cords were not mnemonic and that the beads, feathers, knots, etc., attached to them were not for the purpose of recalling to mind some duty to be performed or prayer to be recited.

I was at first inclined to associate these cords with the *quipus* of the Peruvians, and also with the *wampum* of the aborigines of the Atlantic coast, and investigation only confirms this first suspicion. It is true that both the *wampum* and the *quipu* seem to have advanced from their primitive position as "medicine" and attained, ethnologically speaking, the higher plane of a medium for facilitating exchange or disseminating information, and for that reason their incorporation in this chapter might be objected to by the hypercritical; but a careful perusal of all the notes upon the subject cannot fail to convince the reader that the use of just such medicine cords prevailed all over the world, under one form or another, and has survived to our own times.

In this chapter I will insert notes showing the use of such cords by other tribes, and follow with descriptions of the uses to which the cords of St. Francis and others were put, and with references to the rosaries of different races or different creeds; finally, I will remark upon the superstitions connected with cords, belts, and strings, knotted or unknotted, made of serpent skin, human skin, or human hair. The strangest thing about it all is that observers have, with scarcely an exception, contented themselves with noting the existence of such cords without making the slightest effort to determine why they were used.

There are certain cords with medicine bags attached to be seen in the figures of medicine men in the drawings of the sacred altars given by Matthews in his account of the Navajo medicine-men.

Gushing also has noted the existence of such cords in Zuñi, and there is no doubt that some at least of the so-called "fishing lines" found in the Rio Verde cliff dwellings in Arizona were used for the same purposes.

Describing the tribes met on the Rio Colorado, in 1540-1541, Alarcon says:

> Likewise on the brawne of their armes they weare a streit string, which they wind so often about that it becommeth as broad as one's hand.

It must be remembered that the Indians thought that Alarcon was a god, that they offered sacrifice to him, and that they wore all the "medicine" they possessed.

In 1680, the Pueblos, under the leadership of Pope, of the *pueblo* of San Juan, were successful in their attempt to throw off the Spanish yoke. He made them believe that he was in league with the spirits, and:

> . . . . . that they directed him to make a rope of the palm leaf and tie in it a number of knots to represent the number of days before the rebellion was to take place; that he must send this rope to all the Pueblos in the kingdom, when each should signify its approval of and union with, the conspiracy by untying one of the knots.—Davis, *Conquest of New Mexico.*

I suspect that this may have been an *izze-kloth*. We know nothing about this rebellion excepting what has been derived through Spanish sources; the conquerors despised the natives, and, with a very few notable exceptions among the Franciscans, made no effort to study their peculiarities. The discontent of the natives was aggravated by this fact; they saw their idols pulled down, their ceremonial chambers closed, their dances prohibited, and numbers of their people tried and executed for witchcraft. Fray Geronimo de Zarate Saltneron was a striking example of the good to be effected by missionaries who are not above studying their people; he acquired a complete mastery of the language of the *pueblo* of Jemez, "and preached to the inhabitants in their native tongue."

He is represented as exercising great influence over the people of Jemez, Sia, Santa Ana, and Acoma. In this rebellion of 1080 the Pueblos expected to be joined by the Apache.—Davis.

The *izze-kloth* of the Apache seems to have had its prototype in the sacred string of beans with which Tecumseh's brother, the Shawnee prophet, travelled among the Indian tribes, inciting them to war. Every young warrior who agreed to go upon the warpath touched this "sacred string of beans" in token of his solemn pledge.—Catlin, *North American Indians.*

Tanner says in the narrative of his captivity among the Ojibwa:

> He [the medicine-man] then gave me a small hoop of wood to wear on my head like a cap. On one-half of this hoop was marked the figure of a snake, whose office, as the chief told me, was to take care of the water.

The "small hoop of wood" of which Tanner speaks, to be worn on the head, seems to be analogous to the small hoop attached to the *izze-kloth*, to be worn or applied in cases of headache (Fig. 2). Reference to something very much like the *izze-kloth* is made by Harmon as in use among the Carriers of British North America. He says:

> The lads, as soon as they come to the age of puberty, tie cords, wound with swan's down, around each leg a little below the knee, which they wear during one year, and then they are considered as men.

When I first saw the medicine cords of the Apache, it occurred to me that perhaps in some way they might be an inheritance from the Franciscans, who, two centuries ago, had endeavoured to plant missions among the Apache, and did succeed in doing something for the Navajo part of the tribe. I therefore examined the most convenient authorities and learned that the cord of St. François, like the cord of St. Augustine and the cord of St. Monica, was itself a medicine cord, representing a descent from a condition of thought perfectly parallel to that which has given birth to the *izze-kloth*.

Rosaries and Other Mnemonic Cords.

During the years of my service with the late Maj. Gen. Crook in the Southwest, I was surprised to discover that the Apache scouts kept records of the time of their absence on campaign. There were several methods in vogue, the best being that of coloured beads, which were strung on a string, six white ones to represent the days of the week and one black or other colour to stand for Sundays. This method gave rise to some confusion, because the Indians had been told that there were four weeks, or Sundays ("*Domingos*"), in each "*Luna*," or moon, and yet they soon found that their own method of determining time by the appearance of the crescent moon was much the more satisfactory.

Among the Zuñi I have seen little tally sticks with the marks for the days and months incised on the narrow edges, and among the Apache another method of indicating the flight of time by marking on a piece of paper along a horizontal line a number of circles or of straight lines across the horizontal datum line to represent the full days which had passed, a heavy straight line for each Sunday, and a small crescent for the beginning of each month.

Farther to the south, in the Mexican state of Sonora, I was shown, some twenty years ago, a piece of buckskin, upon which certain Opata or Yaqui Indians—I forget exactly which tribe, but it matters very little, as they are both industrious and honest had kept account of the days of their labor. There was a horizontal *datum* line, as before, with complete circles to indicate full days and half circles to indicate half days, a long heavy black line for Sundays and holidays, and a crescent moon for each new month. These accounts had to be drawn up by the overseer or superintendent of the *rancho* at which the Indians were employed before the latter left for home each night.

"Medidas," "Measuring Cords," "Wresting Threads," etc.

The views of Furlong have been presented, showing that there were reasons for believing that the sacred cords of the East Indies could be traced back to an ophic origin, and it has also been shown that, until the present day, among the peasantry of Europe, there has obtained the practice of making girdles of snake skin which have been employed for the cure of disease and as an assistance in childbirth. The snake itself, while still alive, as has been shown, is applied to the person of the patient by the medicine-men of the American Indians.

In connection with the remarks taken from Forlong's *Rivers of Life* on this subject, I should like to call attention to the fact that the long knotted blacksnake whip of the wagoners of Europe and America, which, when not in use, is worn across the body from shoulder to hip, has been identified as related to snake worship.

There is another view to take of the origin of these sacred cords which it is fair to submit before passing final judgment. The *izze-kloth* may have been in early times a cord for tying captives who were taken in war, and as these captives were offered up in sacrifice to the gods of war and others they were looked upon as sacred, and all used in connection with them would gradually take on a sacred character. The same kind of cords seem to have been used in the chase. This would explain a great deal of the superstition connected with the whole subject of "hangman's rope" bringing luck, curing disease, and averting trouble of all sorts, a superstition more widely disseminated and going back to more ancient times than most people would imagine. One of the tribes of New Granada, "*quando iban à la Guerra Hevaban Cordeles para atar à los Presos.*" This recalls that the Apache themselves used to throw lariats from ambush upon travellers, and that the Thugs who served the goddess Bhowani, in India, strangled with cords, afterwards with handkerchiefs.

THE MEDICINE HAT.

The medicine hat of the old and blind Apache medicine-man, Nan-ta do-tash, was an antique affair of buckskin, much begrimed with soot and soiled by long use. Nevertheless, it gave life and strength to him who wore it, enabled the owner to peer into the future, to tell who had stolen ponies from other people, to foresee the approach of an enemy, and to aid in the cure of the sick. This was its owner's own statement in conversation with me, but it would seem that the power residing in the helmet or hat was not very permanent, because when the old man discovered from his wife that I had made a rude drawing of it he became extremely excited and said that such a delineation would destroy all the life of the hat. His fears were allayed by presents of money and tobacco, as well as by some cakes and other food. As a measure of precaution, he insisted upon sprinkling pinches of *hodden-tin* over myself, the hat, and the drawing of it, at the same time muttering various half-articulate prayers. He returned a mouth afterwards

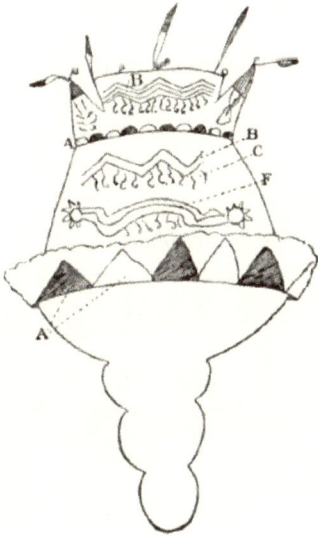

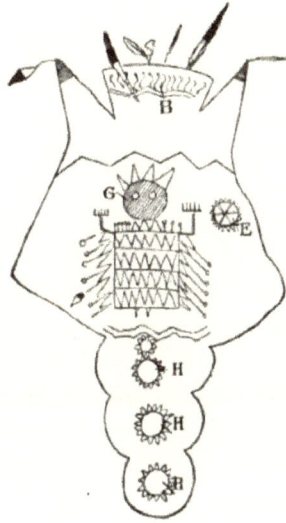

Nan-ta-do-tash's medicine hat.

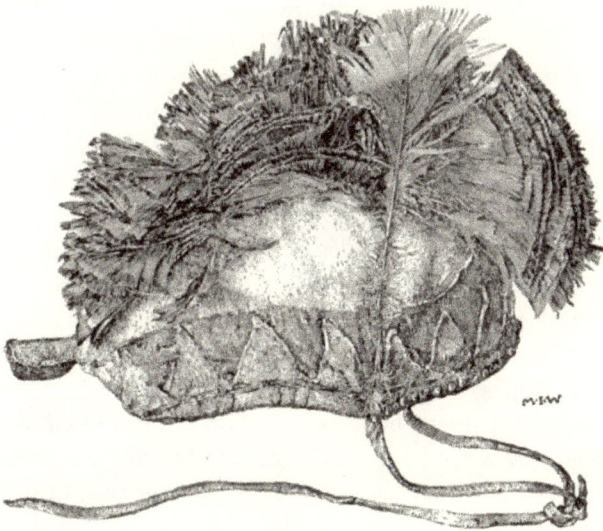

Apache war bonnet.

and demanded the sum of $30 for damage done to the hat by the drawing, since which time it has ceased to "work" when needed.

This same old man gave me an explanation of all the symbolism depicted upon the hat and a great deal of valuable information in regard to the profession of medicine-men, their specialization, the prayers they recited, etc. The material of the hat, as already stated, was buckskin. How that was obtained I cannot assert positively, but from an incident occurring under my personal observation in the Sierra Madre in Mexico in 1883, where our Indian scouts and the medicine-men with them surrounded a nearly grown fawn and tried to capture it alive, as well as from other circumstances too long to be here inserted, I am of the opinion that the buckskin to be used for sacred purposes among the Apache must, whenever possible, be that of a strangled animal, as is the case, according to Dr. Matthews, among the Navajo.

The body of Nau-ta-do-tash's cap was unpainted, but the figures upon it were in two colours, a brownish yellow and an earthy blue, resembling a dirty Prussian blue. The ornamentation was of the downy feathers and black-tipped plumes of the eagle, pieces of abalone shell, and *chalchihuitl*, and a snake's rattle on the apex.

Nan-ta-do-tash explained that the characters on the medicine hat meant: A, clouds; B, rainbow; C, hail; E, morning star; F, the God of Wind, with his lungs; G, the black "*kan*"; H, great stars or suns.

"*Kan*" is the name given to their principal gods. The appearance of the *kan* himself and of the tail of the hat suggest the centipede, an important animal god of the Apache. The old man said that the figures represented the powers to which he appealed for aid in his "medicine" and the *kan* upon whom he called for help. There were other doctors with other medicines, but he used none but those of which he was going to speak to me.

When an Apache or other medicine-man is in full regalia he ceases to be a man, but becomes, or tries to make his followers believe that he has become, the power he represents. I once heard this asserted in a very striking way while I was with a party of Apache young men who had led me to one of the sacred caves of their people, in which we came across a great quantity of ritualistic paraphernalia of all sorts.

"We used to stand down here," they said, "and look up to the top of the mountain and see the *kan* come down." This is precisely what the people living farther to the south told the early Spanish missionaries.

GHOST-DANCE HEADDRESS.

The ghost dance headdress illustrated is known to the Chiricahua Apache as the "*ich-te*," a contraction from "*chas-a-i-wit-te*," according to Ramon, the old medicine-man from whom I obtained it. He explained all the symbolism connected with it. The round piece of tin in the centre is the sun; the irregular arch underneath it is the rainbow. Stars and lightning are depicted on the side slats and under them; the parallelograms with serrated edges are clouds; the pendant green sticks are rain drops; there are snakes and snake heads on both horizontal and vertical slats, the heads in the former case being representative of hail.

There are feathers of the eagle to conciliate that powerful bird, turkey feathers to appeal to the mountain spirits, and white gull feathers for the spirits of the water. There are also small pieces of nacreous shells and one or two fragments of the "*duklij*," or *chalchihuitl*, without which no medicine-man would feel competent to discharge his functions.

The spirit dance itself is called "*cha-ja-la*." I have seen this dance a number of times, but will confine my description to one seen at Fort Marion (St. Augustine, Fla.), in 1887, when the Chiricahua Apache were confined there as prisoners; although the accompanying figure represents a ghost dance headdress seen among the Apache in the winter of 1885. A great many of the band had been suffering from sickness of one kind or another and twenty-three of the children had died; as a consequence, the medicine-men were having the *Cha-ja-la*, which is entered into only upon the most solemn occasions, such as the setting out of a war party, the appearance of an epidemic, or something else of like portent.

On the *terreplein* of the northwest bastion, Ramon, the old medicine-man, was violently beating upon a drum, which, as usual, had been improvised of a soaped rag drawn tightly over the mouth of an iron kettle holding a little water.

Although acting as master of ceremonies, Ramon was not painted or decorated in any way. Three other medicine-men were having the finishing touches put to their bodily decoration. They had an under-coating of greenish brown, and on each arm a yellow snake, the head toward the shoulder blade. The snake on the arm of one of the party was double-headed, or rather had a head at each extremity.

Each had insignia in yellow on back and breast, but no two were exactly alike. One had on his breast a yellow bear, 4 inches long by 3 inches high, and on his back a *kan* of the same colour and dimensions. A second had the same pattern of bear on his breast, but a zigzag for lightning on his back. The third had the zigzag on both back and breast. All wore kilts and *moccasins*.

While the painting was going on Ramon thumped and sang with vigour to insure the medicinal potency of the pigments and the designs to which they were applied. Each held, one in each hand, two wands or swords of lathlike proportions, ornamented with snake-lightning in blue.

The medicine-men emitted a peculiar whistling noise and bent slowly to the right, then to the left, then frontward, then backward, until the head in each case was level with the waist. Quickly they spun round in full circle on the left foot; back again in a reverse circle to the right; then they charged around the little group of tents in that bastion, making cuts and thrusts with their wands to drive the maleficent spirits away.

It recalled to my mind the old myths of the angel with the flaming sword guarding the entrance to Eden, or of St. Michael chasing the discomfited Lucifer down into the depths of Hell.

These preliminaries occupied a few moments only; at the end of that time the medicine-men advanced to where a squaw was holding up to them a little baby sick in its cradle. The mother remained kneeling while the medicine-men frantically struck at, upon, around, and over the cradle with their wooden weapons.

The baby was held so as successively to occupy each of the cardinal points and face each point directly opposite; first on the east side, facing the west; then the north side, facing the south; then the west side, facing the east; then the south side, facing the north, and back to the original position. While at each position, each of the medicine-men in succession, after making all the passes and gestures described, seized the cradle in his hands, pressed it to his breast, and afterwards lifted it up to the sky, next to the earth, and lastly to the four cardinal points, all the time prancing, whistling, and snorting, the mother and her squaw friends adding to the dismal din by piercing shrieks and ululations.

That ended the ceremonies for that night so far as the baby personally was concerned, but the medicine-men retired down to the parade and resumed their saltation, swinging, bending, and spinning with such violence that they resembled, in a faint way perhaps, the Dervishes of the East. The understanding was that the dance had to be kept up as long as there was any fuel unconsumed of the large pile provided; any other course would entail bad luck. It was continued for four nights, the colours and the symbols upon the bodies varying from night to night. Among the modes of exorcism enumerated by Burton, we find "cutting the air with swords." Picart speaks of the "*flêches ou les baguettes dont les Arabes Idolâltres se servoient pour deviner par le sort.*" (Arrows or sticks that the idolatrous Arabs were using to guess the fate). He says that the diviner "*tenoit a la main*" (held in his hand), these arrows, which certainly suggest the swords or wands of the Apache medicine-men in the spirit dance.

There were four medicine-men, three of whom were dancing and in conference with the spirits, and the fourth of whom was general superintendent of the whole dance, and the authority to whom the first three reported the result of their interviews with the ghostly powers.

The mask and headdress of the first of the dancers, who seemed to be the leading one, was so elaborate that in the hurry and meagre light supplied by the flickering fires it could not be portrayed. It was very much like that of number three, but so fully covered with the plumage of the eagle, hawk, and, apparently, the owl, that it was difficult to assert this positively. Each of these medicine-men had pieces of red flannel tied to his elbows and a stick about four feet long in each hand. Number one's mask was spotted black and white and shaped in front like the snout of a mountain lion. His back was painted with large arrowheads in brown and white, which recalled the protecting arrows tightly bound to the backs of Zuñi fetishes. Number two had on his back a figure in white ending between the shoulders in a cross. Number three's back was simply whitened with clay.

All these headdresses were made of slats of the Spanish bayonet, unpainted, excepting that on number two was a figure in black, which could not be made out, and that the horizontal crosspieces on number three were painted blue.

The *dominos* or masks were of blackened buckskin, for the two fastened around the neck by garters or sashes; the neckpiece of number three was painted red; the eyes seemed to be glass knobs or brass buttons. These three dancers were naked to the waist, and wore beautiful kilts of fringed buckskin bound on with sashes, and *moccasins* reaching to the knees. In this guise they jumped into the centre of the great circle of spectators and singers and began running about the fire shrieking and muttering, encouraged by the shouts and the singing, and by the drumming and incantation of the chorus which now swelled forth at full lung power.

The Spirit of Ghost Dance Headdress.

As the volume of music swelled and the cries of the onlookers became fiercer, the dancers were encouraged to the enthusiasm of frenzy. They darted about the circle, going through the motions of looking for an enemy, all the while muttering, mumbling, and singing, jumping, swaying, and whirling like the dancing *dervishes* of Arabia.

Their actions, at times, bore a very considerable resemblance to the movements of the Zuñi Shálako at the Feast of Fire. Klashidn told me that the orchestra was singing to the four willow branches planted near them. This would indicate a vestige of tree worship, such as is to be noticed also at the sun dance of the Sioux.

At intervals, the three dancers would dart out of the ring and disappear in the darkness, to consult with the spirits or with other medicine-men seated a considerable distance from the throng. Three several times they appeared and disappeared, always dancing, running, and whirling about with increased energy. Having attained the degree of mental or spiritual exaltation necessary for communion with the spirits, they took their departure and kept away for at least half an hour, the orchestra during their absence rendering a mournful refrain, monotonous as a funeral dirge. My patience became exhausted and I turned to go to my quarters. A thrill of excited expectancy ran through the throng of Indians, and I saw that they were looking anxiously at the returning medicine-men. All the orchestra now stood up, their leader (the principal medicine-man) slightly in advance, holding a branch of cedar in his left hand. The first advanced and bending low his head murmured some words of unknown import with which the chief seemed to be greatly pleased.

Then the chief, taking his stand in front of the orchestra on the east side of the grove or cluster of trees, awaited the final ceremony, which

APACHE KAN OR GODS. (DRAWN BY APACHE.)

APACHE MEDICINE HAT
USED IN GHOST DANCE.

was as follows: The three dancers in file and in proper order advanced and receded three times; then they embraced the chief in such a manner that the sticks or wands held in their hands came behind his neck, after which they mumbled and muttered a jumble of sounds which I cannot reproduce, but which sounded for all the world like the chant of the "hooter" at the Zuñi Feast of Fire.

They then pranced or danced through the grove three times. This was repeated for each point of the compass, the chief medicine-man, with the orchestra, taking a position successively on the east, south, west, and north and the three dancers advancing, receding, and embracing as at first. This terminated the "medicine" ceremonies of the evening, the glad shouts of the Apache testifying that the incantations of their spiritual leaders or their necromancy, whichever it was, promised a successful campaign. These dancers were, I believe, dressed up to represent their gods or *kan*, but not content with representing them aspired to be mistaken for them.

AMULETS AND TALISMANS
THE "TZI-DALTAI."

The Apache, both men and women, wear amulets, called *tzi-daltai*, made of lightning-riven wood, generally pine or cedar or fir from the mountain tops, which are highly valued and are not to be sold. These are shaved very thin and rudely cut in the semblance of the human form. They are in fact the duplicates, on a small scale, of the rhombus, already described. Like the rhombus, they are decorated with incised lines representing the lightning. Very often these are to be found attached to the necks of children or to their cradles. Generally these amulets are of small size.

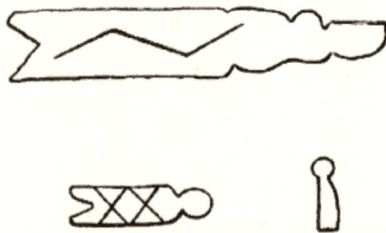

FIG 1 TZI-DALTAI AMULET (APACHE)

Below will be found figures of those which I was permitted to examine and depict. They are all unpainted.

The amulet represented was obtained from a Chiricahua Apache captive. Deguele, an Apache of the Klukaydakaydn clan, consented to exhibit a *kan*, or god, which he carried about his person. He said I could have it for three ponies. It was made of a flat piece of lath, unpainted, of the size here given, having drawn upon it this figure in yellow, with a narrow black band, excepting the three snake heads, *a*, *b*, and *c*, which were black with white eyes; *a* was a yellow line and *c* a black line; flat pearl buttons were fastened at *m* and *k* respectively and small eagle-down feathers at *k* on each side of the idol. The rear of the tablet, amulet, or idol, as one may be pleased to call it, was almost an exact reproduction of the front.

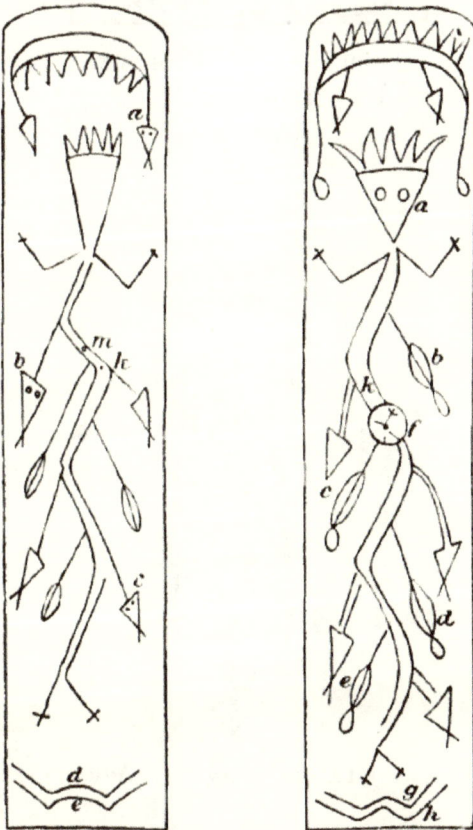

Front view.   Rear view.

Fig. 2. Tzi-daltai amulet (Apache).

Front view.   Rear view.

FIG 3. Tzi-daltai amulet
(Apache).

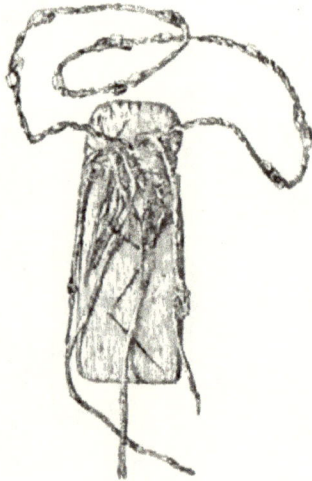

FIG. 4. Tzi-daltai amulet (Apache).

The owner of this inestimable treasure assured me that he prayed to it at all timeswhen in trouble, that he could learn from it where his ponies were when stolen and which was the right direction to travel when lost, and that when drought had parched his crops this would never fail to bring rain in abundance to revive and strengthen them. The symbolism is the rain cloud and the serpent lightning, the rain-bow, rain drops, and the cross of the four winds.

These small amulets are also to be found inclosed in the phylacter-ies (see sketch) which the medicine-men wear suspended from their necks or waists.

CHALCHIHUITL.

The articles of dress depicted in this book are believed to represent all those which exclusively belong to the office of the Apache "*diyi*" or "*izze-nantan*." Of late years it cannot be said that every medicine-man has all these articles, but most of them will be found in the possession of the man in full practice.

No matter what the medicine-man may lack, he will, if it be pos-sible, provide himself with some of the impure malachite known to the whites of the Southwest as turquoise. In the malachite veins the latter stone is sometimes found and is often of good quality, but the difference between the two is apparent upon the slightest examina-tion. The colour of the malachite is a pea green, that of the turquoise a pale sky blue. The chemical composition of the former is a carbonate of copper, mixed with earthy impurities; that of the latter, a phosphate of alumina, coloured with the oxide of copper.

The use of this malachite was widespread. Under the name of *chalchihuitl* or *chalchihuite*, it appears with frequency in the old Spanish writings, as we shall presently see, and was in all places and by all tribes possessing it revered in much the same manner as by the Apache. The Apache call it *duklij.*, "blue (or green) stone," these two colours not being differentiated in their language.

A small bead of this mineral affixed to a gun or bow made the weapon shoot accurately. It had also some relation to the bringing of rain, and could be found by the man who would go to the end of a rainbow, after a storm, and hunt diligently in the damp earth. It was the Apache medicine-man's badge of office, his medical diploma, so to speak, and without it he could not in olden times exercise his medical functions. In the curious commerce of the Indian tribes, some pos-sessed articles of greater worth than those belonging to their neigh-

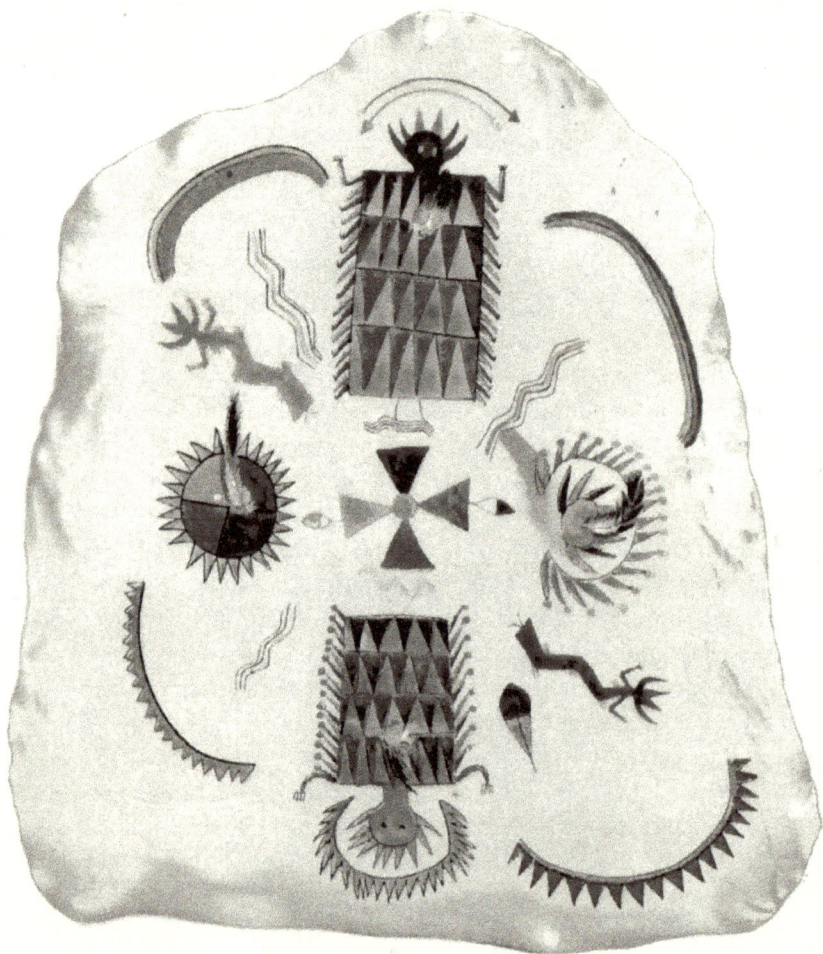

APACHE MEDICINE SHIRT.

bors. In the southwest the red paint sold by the tribes living in the Grand Canyon of the Colorado was held in higher repute than any other, and the green stone to be purchased from the Rio Grande Pueblos always was in great demand, as it is to this day. Vetancurt speaks of the Apache, between the years 1630 and 1680, coming to the *pueblo* of Pecos to trade for "chalchihuites." John de Laet speaks of "*petites pierres verdes,*" (small green stones), worn in the lower lip by the Brazilians.

PHYLACTERIES.

The term phylactery, as herein employed, means any piece of buckskin or other material upon which are inscribed certain characters or symbols of a religious or "medicine" nature, which slip or phylactery is to be worn attached to the person seeking to be benefited by it, and this phylactery differs from the amulet or talisman in being concealed from the scrutiny of the profane and kept as secret as possible, This phylactery, itself "medicine," may be employed to enwrap other "medicine" and thus augment its own potentiality. Indians in general object to having their "medicine" scrutinized and touched; in this there is a wide margin of individual opinion; but in regard to phylacteries there is none that I have been able to discover, and the rule may be given as antagonistic to the display of these sacred "relics," as my Mexican captive interpreter persisted in calling them.

The first phylactery which it was my good fortune to be allowed to examine was one worn by Ta-ul-tzu-je, of the Kaytzentin gens. It was tightly rolled in at least half a mile of orange-coloured saddlers' silk, obtained from some of the cavalry posts. After being duly uncovered, it was found to be a small piece of buckskin two inches square, upon which were drawn red and yellow crooked lines which the Apache said represented the red and yellow snake. Inside were a piece of green *chalchihuitl* and a small cross of lightning-riven twig (pine) and two very small perforated shells. The cross was called "*intchi-dijin*," the black wind.

A second phylactery which I was also allowed to untie and examine belonged to Na-a-cha and consisted of a piece of buckskin of the same size as the other, but either on account of age or for some other reason no characters could be discerned upon it. It, however, enwrapped a tiny bag of *hoddentin*, which, in its turn, held a small but very clear crystal of quartz and four feathers of eagle down. Na-a-cha took care to explain very earnestly that this phylactery contained not merely the "medicine" or power of the crystal, the *hoddentin*, and the

Yellow. Yellow.

Red. Red.

Red. Red.

Yellow. Yellow.

Shell.

Eagle Down.

PHYLACTERIES.

itza-chu, or eagle, but also of the *shoz-dijiji*, or black bear, the *shoz-le-kay*, or white bear, the *shoz-litzogue*, or yellow bear, and the *klij-litzogue* or yellow snake, though just in what manner he could not explain.

It would take up too much time and space to describe the manner in which it was necessary for me to proceed in order to obtain merely a glimpse of these and other phylacteries, all of the same general type; how I had to make it evident that I was myself possessed of great "medicine" power and able to give presents of great "medicine" value, as was the case. I had obtained from cliff dwellings, sacred caves, and other places beads of talc, of *chalchihuitl*, and of shell, pieces of crystal and other things, sacred in the eyes of the Apache, and these I was compelled to barter for the information here given.

The medicine shirts of the Apaches, several of which are here represented, do not require an extended description. The symbolism is different for each one, but may be generalized as typical of the sun, moon, stars, rainbow, lightning, snake, clouds, rain, hail, tarantula, centipede, snake, and some one or more of the "*kan*" or gods.

The medicine sashes follow closely in pattern the medicine shirts, being smaller in size only, but with the same symbolic decoration. Similar ornamentation will be found upon the amulets (*ditzi*), made of lightning-struck pine or other wood. All of these are warranted, among other virtues, to screen the wearer from the arrows, lances, or bullets of the enemy. In this they strongly resemble the salves and other means by which people in Europe sought to obtain "magical impenetrability." The last writer to give receipts for making such salves, etc., that I can recall, was Etmüller, who wrote in the early years of the seventeenth century.

APACHE MEDICINE SASH.

Such as the reader can imagine the medicine-man to be from this description of his paraphernalia, such he has been since the white man first landed in America. Never desirous of winning proselytes to his own ideas, he has held on to those ideas with a tenacity never suspected until purposely investigated. The first of the Spanish writers seem to have employed the native terms for the medicine-men, and we come across them as *cemis* or *zemis*, *bohiti*, *pachnaci*, and others; but soon they were recognized as the emissaries of Satan and the preachers of witchcraft, and henceforth they appear in the documents as "*hechicheros*" and "*brujos*" almost exclusively. "*Tienan los Apaches profetas ó adivinos que gozan de la mas alta estimacion. Esos adivinos pratican la medicina lamas rudimental, la aplicacion de algunas yerbas y esto acompanado de ceremonias y cantos supersticiosos.*" (Apaches have prophets or fortune tellers that enjoy the highest esteem. These soothsayers practice rudimentary medicine, the application of some herbs coupled with superstitious ceremonies and songs.) Pimentel seems to have derived his information from Cordero, a Spanish officer who had served against the Apache at various times between 1770 and 1795, and seemed to understand them well.

> There was no class of persons who so widely and deeply influenced the culture and shaped the destiny of the Indian tribes as their priests. In attempting to gain a true conception of the race's capacities and history there is no one element of their social life which demands closer attention than the power of these teachers. . . . However much we may deplore the use they made of their skill, we must estimate it fairly and grant it its due weight in measuring the influence of the religious sentiment on the history of man.—Brinton, *Myths of the New World.*

> Like Old Men of the Sea, they have clung to the neck of their nations, throttling all attempts at progress, binding them to the thraldom of superstition and profligacy, dragging them down to wretchedness and death. Christianity and civilization meet in them their most determined, most implacable foes.—Brinton.

It will only be after we have thoroughly routed the medicine-men from their intrenchments and made them an object of ridicule that we can hope to bend and train the mind of our Indian wards in the direction of civilization. In my own opinion, the reduction of the medicine-men will effect more for the savages than the giving of land in severalty or instruction in the schools at Carlisle and Hampton;

APACHE MEDICINE SHIRT.

rather, the latter should be conducted with this great object mainly in view: to let pupils insensibly absorb such knowledge as may soonest and most completely convince them of the impotency of the charlatans who hold the tribes in bondage.

Teach the scholars at Carlisle and Hampton some of the wonders of electricity, magnetism, chemistry, the spectroscope, magic lantern, ventriloquism, music, and then, when they return to their own people, each will despise the fraud of the medicine-men and be a focus of growing antagonism to their pretensions. Teach them to love their own people and not to despise them; but impress upon each one that he is to return as a missionary of civilization. Let them see that the world is free to the civilized, that law is liberty.

The Urine Dance of the Zuni Indians of New Mexico

On the evening of November 17, 1881, during my stay in the village of Zuni, New Mexico, the *Nehue-Cue*, one of secret orders of the Zunis, sent word to Mr. F. Cushing (whose guest I was) that they would do us the unusual honour of coming to our house to give us one of their characteristic dances, which, Cushing said, was unprecedented.

The squaws of the governor's family put the long "living room" to rights, sweeping the floor and sprinkling it with water to lay the dust. Soon after dark the dancers entered; they were twelve in number, two being boys. The centre men were naked with the exception of black breech-clouts of archaic style. The hair was worn naturally with a bunch of wild turkey feathers tied in front, and one of corn-husks over each ear. White bands were painted across the face at eyes and mouth. Each wore a collar or neckcloth of black woollen stuff. Broad white bands, one inch wide, were painted around the body at the navel, around the arms, the legs at mid-thighs and knees. Tortoise-shell rattles hung from the right knee. Blue woollen footless *leggins* were worn with low-cut *moccasins*, and in the right hand each waved a wand made of an ear of corn, trimmed with the plumage of the wild turkey and macaw.

The others were arrayed in old cast-off American army clothing, and all wore white cotton night-caps, with corn-husks twisted into the hair at top of head and ears. Several wore, in addition to the tortoise-shell rattles, strings of brass sleigh-bells at knees. One was more grotesquely attired than the rest in a long India-rubber gossamer "over all" and a pair of goggles, painted white, over his eyes. His general "get-up" was a spirited take-off upon a Mexican priest. Another was

107

a very good counterfeit of a young woman.

To the accompaniment of an oblong drum, and of the rattles and bells spoken of, they shuffled into the long room, crammed with spectators of both sexes, and of all sizes and ages. Their song was apparently a ludicrous reference to everything and everybody in sight, Cushing, Mendeleff, and myself receiving special attention, to the uncontrolled merriment of the red-skinned listeners. I had taken my station at one side of the room, seated upon the *banquette*, and having in front of me a rude bench or table upon which was a small coal-oil lamp. I suppose that in the halo diffused by the feeble light and in my "stained-glass attitude" I must have borne some resemblance to the pictures of saints hanging upon the walls of old Mexican churches; to such a fancied resemblance I at least attribute the performance which followed.

The dancers suddenly wheeled into line, threw themselves on their knees before my table, and with extravagant beatings of breast began an outlandish but faithful mockery of a Mexican Catholic congregation at vespers. One bawled out a parody upon the *Pater Noster*, another mumbled along in the manner of an old man reciting the rosary, while the fellow with the India-rubber coat jumped up and began a passionate exhortation or sermon, which for mimetic fidelity was inimitable. This kept the audience laughing with sore sides for some moments, until at a signal from the leader the dancers suddenly countermarched out of the room, in single file, as they had entered.

An interlude followed of ten minutes, during which the dusty floor was sprinkled by men who spat water forcibly from their mouths. The *Nehue-Cue* re-entered; this time two of their number were stark naked. Their singing was very peculiar and sounded like a chorus of chimney-sweeps, and their dance became a stiff-legged jump, with heels kept twelve inches apart. After they had ambled around the room two or three times, Cushing announced in the Zuni language that a "feast" was ready for them, at which they loudly roared their approbation and advanced to strike hands with the munificent *Americanos*, addressing us in a funny gibberish of broken Spanish, English, and Zuni. They then squatted upon the ground and consumed with zest large *ollas* full of tea, and dishes of hard tack and sugar. As they were about finishing this a squaw entered, carrying an *olla* of urine, of which the filthy brutes drank heartily.

I refused to believe the evidence of my senses, and asked Cushing if that were really human urine. "Why, certainly," replied he, "and here comes more of it." This time, it was a large tin-pailfull, not less than two gallons. I was standing by the squaw as she offered this strange and abominable refreshment. She made a motion with her hand to indicate to me that it was urine, and one of the old men repeated the Spanish word *mear* (to urinate), while my sense of smell demonstrated the truth of their statements.

The dancers swallowed great draughts, smacked their lips, and, amid the roaring merriment of the spectators, remarked that it was very, very good. The clowns were now upon their mettle, each trying to surpass his neighbours in feats of nastiness. One swallowed a fragment of corn-husk, saying he thought it very good and better than bread; his *vis-à-vis* attempted to chew and gulp down a piece of filthy rag. Another expressed regret that the dance had not been held out of doors, in one of the *plazas*; there they could show what they could do. There they always made it a point of honour to eat the excrement of men and dogs.

For my own part I felt satisfied with the omission, particularly as the room, stuffed with one hundred Zunis, had become so foul and filthy as to be almost unbearable. The dance, as good luck would have it, did not last many minutes, and we soon had a chance to run into the refreshing night air.

To this outline description of a disgusting rite I have little to add. The Zunis, in explanation, stated that the *Nehue-Cue* were a Medicine Order which held these dances from time to time to inure the stomachs of members to any kind of food, no matter how revolting. This statement may seem plausible enough when we understand that religion and medicine among primitive races are almost always one and the same thing, or, at least, so closely intertwined that it is a matter of difficulty to decide where one begins and the other ends.

Religion in its dramatic ceremonial preserves, to some extent, the history of the particular race in which it dwells. Among nations of high development, miracles, moralities, and passion plays have taught, down to our own day, in object lessons, the sacred history in which the spectators believed. Some analogous purpose may have been held in view by the first organizers of the urine dance. In their early history, the Zunis and other Pueblos suffered from constant warfare with savage antagonists and with each other. From the position of their villages, long sieges must of necessity have been sustained, in which sieges famine and disease, no doubt, were the allies counted upon by the investing forces. We may have in this abominable dance a tradition of the extremity to which the Zunis of the long ago were reduced at some unknown period.

A similar catastrophe in the history of the Jews is intimated in II Kings, xviii, 27:

But Rab-shakeh said unto them: hath my master sent me to thy master, and to thee to speak these words? hath he not sent me to the men which sit on the wall, that they may eat their own dung and drink their own piss with you?

In the course of my studies, I came across a reference to a very similar dance, occurring among one of the fanatical sects of the Arabian Bedouins, but the journal in which it was recorded, the *London Lancet*, I think, was unfortunately mislaid.

As illustrative of the tenacity with which such vile ceremonial, once adopted by a sect, will adhere to it and become ingrafted upon its life, long after the motives which have suggested or commended it have vanished in oblivion, let me quote a few lines from Max Muller's *Chips from a German Workshop*, "Essay upon the Parsees," pp. 163, 164, Scribner's edition, 1869:

The *Nirang* is the urine of cow, ox, or she-goat, and the rubbing of it over the face and hands is the second thing a Parsee does after getting out of bed. Either before applying the *Nirang* to the face and hands, or while it remains on the hands after being applied, he should not touch anything directly with his hands; but, in order to wash out the *Nirang*, he either asks somebody else to pour water on his hands, or resorts to the device of taking hold of the pot through the intervention of a piece of cloth, such as a handkerchief, or his *sudra*, *i.e.*, his blouse. He first pours water on his hand, then takes the pot in that hand and washes his other hand, face, and feet. (Quoting from *Dadabhai-Nadrosi's* Description of the Parsees.)

Continuing, Max Muller says:

Strange as this process of purification may appear, it becomes perfectly disgusting when we are told that women, after childbirth, have not only to undergo this sacred ablution, but actually to drink a little of the *Nirangj* and that the same rite is imposed on children at the time of their investiture with the *Sudra* and *Koshti*, the badges of the Zoroastrian faith.

The Use of Human Ordure and Human Urine in Rites of a Religious or Semi-Religious Character

All that Higgins believed was believed and asserted by the Dominican missionary Diego Duran. Duran complains bitterly that the unwise destruction of the ancient Mexican pictographs and all that explained the religion of the natives left the missionaries in ignorance as to what was religion and what was not. The Indians, taking advantage of this, mocked and ridiculed the dogmas and ceremonies of the new creed in the very face of its expounders, who still lacked a complete mastery of the language of the conquered. The Indians never could be induced to admit that they still adhered to their old superstitions, or that they were boldly indulging in their religious observances; many times, says the shrewd old chronicler, it would appear that they were merely indulging in some pleasant pastime, while they were really engaged in idolatry; or that they were playing games, when truly they were casting lots for future events before the priest's eyes; or that they were subjecting themselves to penitential discipline, when they were sacrificing to their gods.

This remark applied to all that they did. In dances, in baths, in markets, in singing their songs, in their dramas (the word is "*comedia*," a comedy, but a note in the margin of the manuscript says that probably this ought to be "*comida*," food, or dinner, or feast), in sowing, in reaping, in putting away the harvest in their granaries, even in tilling the ground, in building their houses, in their funerals, in their burials, in marriages, in the birth of children, into everything they did entered idolatry and superstition.

111

Fray Diego Duran, a Fray Predicador of the Dominican Order, says, at the end of his second volume, that it was finished in 1581.

The very same views were held by Father Geronimo Boscana, a Franciscan, who ministered for seventeen years to the Indians of California. Every act of an Indian's life was guided by religion. (See "Chinigchinich," included in A. A. Robinson's *California*, New York, 1850.)

The Apaches have dances in which the prehistoric condition of the tribe is thus represented; so have the Mojaves and the Zunis; while in the snake dance of the Moquis and the sun dance of the Sioux the same faithful adherence to traditional costume and manners is apparent.

The Urine Dance of the Zunis May Conserve a Tradition of the Time When Vile Aliment Was in Use

The Zuni urine dance may therefore not improperly be considered, among other points of view, under that which suggests a commemoration of the earliest life of this people, when vile aliment of every kind may have been in use through necessity.

An examination of evidence will show that foods now justly regarded as noxious were once not unknown to nations of even greater development than any as yet attained by the Rio Grande Pueblos. Necessity was not always the inciting motive; frequently religious frenzy was responsible for orgies of which only vague accounts and still vaguer explanations have come down to us.

Excrement Used in Human Food.

The very earliest accounts of the Indians of Florida and Texas refer to the use of such aliment. Cabeça de Vaca, one of the survivors of the ill-fated expedition of Panfilo de Narvaez, was a prisoner among various tribes for many years, and finally, accompanied by three comrades as wretched as himself, succeeded in traversing the continent, coming out at Culiacan, on the Pacific coast, in 1536.

His narrative says that the "Floridians for food dug roots, and that they ate spiders, ant's eggs, worms, lizards, salamanders, snakes, earth, wood, the dung of deer, and many other things." The same account, given in *Purchas' Pilgrims* (vol. 4), expresses it that "they also eat earth, wood, and whatever they can get; the dung of wild beasts." These remarks may be understood as applying to all tribes seen by this early explorer east of the Rocky Mountains.

Gómara identifies this loathsome diet with a particular tribe, the

"Yaguaces" of Florida. "They eat spiders, ants, worms, lizards of two kinds, snakes, wood, earth, and ordure of all kinds of wild animals."[1]

The California Indians were still viler. The German Jesuit, Father Jacob Baegert, speaking of the Lower Californians (among whom he resided continuously from 1748 to 1765), says:

> They eat the seeds of the *pitahaya* [giant cactus] which have passed off undigested from their own stomachs; they gather their own excrement, separate the seeds from it, roast, grind, and eat them, making merry over the loathsome meal.

And again:

> In the mission of St. Ignatius .... there are persons who will attach a piece of meat to a string and swallow it and pull it out again a dozen times in succession for the sake of protracting the enjoyment of its taste.—(Translation of Dr. Charles F. Rau, in *Annual Report Smithsonian Institution*, 1866.)

The Indians of British North America, according to Harmon, "boil the buffalo paunch, with much of its dung adhering to it"—a filthy mode of cooking, which in itself would mean little since it can be paralleled in almost all tribes; but, in another paragraph, the same author says, "many consider a broth made by means of the dung of the cariboo and the hare to be a dainty dish." (Harmon's *Journal*, &c., Andover, 1820.)[2]

The Abbé Domenech asserts the same of the bands near Lake Superior:

> In boiling their wild rice to eat they mix it with the excrement of rabbit—a delicacy appreciated by the epicures among them.—(Domenech, *Deserts*, vol. 2.)

BACCHIC ORGIES IN NORTH AMERICA.

These orgies were duplicated among many of the tribes of North America. Paul Kane describes the inauguration of Clea-clach, a Clal-

---

1. He derives his information from the narrative of Vaca. The word "*cagajon*" means horse dung, the dung of mules and asses; "*cagarruta*" the dung of sheep, goats, and mice.
2. Harmon's notes are of special interest at this point, because he is speaking of the Ta-cully or Carriers, who belong to the same Tinneh stock as the Apaches and Navajoes of Arizona and New Mexico. Lipans of Texas. Umpquas of Washington Territory, Hoopahs of California, and Slowcuss of the head-waters of the Columbia River.

lum chief (Northwest coast of British America); "he seized a small dog and began devouring it alive." He also bit pieces from the shoulders of the male bystanders. (See *Artist's Wanderings in North America*, London, 1859; also, the same thing quoted by Herbert Spencer, in *Descriptive Sociology*.)

Bancroft describes like orgies among the Chimsyans, of British North America. (See in *Native Races of the Pacific Slope*, vol. 1.) While the Nootkas medicine-men are said to have an orgie in which "live dogs and dead human bodies are seized and torn by their teeth; but, at least in later times, they seem not to attack the living, and their performances are somewhat less horrible and bloody than the wild orgies of the northern tribes." (*Idem*, vol. 1.)

The Haidahs, of the same coast, indulge in an orgie in which the performer "snatches up the first dog he can find, kills him, and tearing pieces of his flesh, eats them." (Dall, quoting Dawson, in *Masks and Labrets*, Annual Report of the Bureau of Ethnology, Washington, D. C, 1886.)

In describing the six secret soldier societies or bands of the Mandans, Maximilian, of Wied, calls attention to the three leaders of one band, who were called dogs, who are "obliged, if anyone throws a piece of meat into the ashes or on the ground, saying, 'There, dog, eat,' to fall upon it and devour it raw, like dogs or beasts of prey." (Maximilian, Prince of Wied, *Travels*, &c., London, 1843.)

A further multiplication of references is unnecessary. The above would appear to be enough to establish the existence of almost identical orgies in Europe, America, and Asia—orgies in which were perpetuated the ritualistic use of foods no longer employed by the populace, and possibly commemorating a former condition of cannibalism.

THE SACRIFICE OF THE DOG A SUBSTITUTION FOR HUMAN SACRIFICE.

It would add much to the bulk of this chapter to show that the dog has almost invariably been employed as a substitute for man in sacrifice. Other animals have performed the same vicarious office, but none to the same extent, especially among the more savage races. To the American Indians and other peoples of a corresponding stage of development the substitution presents no logical incongruity. Their religious conceptions are so strongly tinged with *zoolatry* that the assignment of animals to the *rôle* of deities or of victims is the most natural thing in the world; but their belief is not limited to the idea that

114

the animal is sacred—it comprehends, additionally, a settled apprecia-
tion of the fact that *lycanthropy* is possible, and that the medicine-men
possess the power of transforming men into animals or animals into
men.

Such a belief was expressed to the writer in the most forcible way,
in the village of Zuni, in 1881. The Indians were engaged in some
one of their countless dances and ceremonies (and possibly not very
far from the time of the urine dance), when the dancers seized a small
dog and tore it limb from limb, venting upon it every torture that
savage spite and malignity could devise. The explanation given was,
that the hapless cur was a "Navajo," a tribe with which the Zunis have
been spasmodically hostile for generations, and from whose ranks the
fortunes of war must have enabled them to drag an occasional captive
to be put to the torture and sacrificed.

Urine in Human Food—Chinook Olives.

The addition of urine to human food is mentioned by various
writers. Speaking of the Chinooks, Paul Kane describes a delicacy
manufactured by some of the Indians among whom he travelled, and
called by him "Chinook olives." They were nothing more or less than
acorns soaked for five months in human urine. (Kane, *Artist's Wanderings in North America*, London, 1859.) Spencer copies Kane's story in
his *Descriptive Sociology*, article "Chinooks."

Urine Used in Bread-Making.

A comparatively late writer says of the Mokis of Arizona:

They are not as clean in their housekeeping as the Navajoes,
and it is hinted that they sometimes mix their meal with cham-
ber-lye for these festive occasions, but I did not know that until
I talked with Mormons who had visited them.—(J. H. Beadle,
Western Wilds, Cincinnati, Ohio, 1878, p. 279.)

Beadle lived and ate with the Mokis for a number of days. This
story, coming from the Mormons, may refer to some imperfectly understood ceremonial.

Poisonous Mushrooms Used in Ur-Orgies.

The Indians in and around Cape Flattery, on the Pacific coast of
British North America, retain the urine dance in an unusually repulsive form. As was learned from Mr. Kennard, U. S. Coast Survey,
whom the writer had the pleasure of meeting in Washington, D. C, in

1886, the medicine men distil, from potatoes and other ingredients, a vile liquor, which has an irritating and exciting effect upon the kidneys and bladder. Each one who has partaken of this dish immediately urinates and passes the result to his next neighbour, who drinks. The effect is as above, and likewise a temporary insanity or delirium, during which all sorts of mad capers are carried on. The last man who quaffs the poison, distilled through the persons of five or six comrades, is so completely overcome that he falls, in a dead stupor.

Mushrooms and Toadstools Worshiped by American Indians.

Dorman is authority for the statement that mushrooms were worshiped by the Indians of the Antilles, and toadstools by those in Virginia,[3] but for what toxic or therapeutic qualities, real or supposed, he does not say.

The Mistletoe Alleged to Have Been Held Sacred by the Mound-Builders.

An American writer says, that among the Mound-builders the mistletoe was "the holiest and most rare of evergreens," and that when human sacrifices were offered to sun and moon the victim was covered with mistletoe, which was burnt as an incense. (Pidgeon, *Dee-coo-dah*, New York, 1853.) Pidgeon claimed to receive his knowledge from Indians versed in the traditions and lore of their tribes.[4]

Mrs. Eastman presents a drawing of what may be taken as the altar of Haokah, the anti-natural God of the Sioux, in which is a representation of a "large fungus that grows on trees" (query, mistletoe?), which, if eaten by an animal, will cause its death,[5]

Dung and Cow Urine in Religion.

The author of this article learned while campaigning with General Crook against the hostile Sioux and Cheyennes in 1876 and 1877 that the Sioux and Assinniboines had a form of oath sworn to while the affiant held in each hand a piece of buffalo chip.

---

3. Rushton M. Dorman, *Primitive Superstitions*, New York, 1881.
4. See also Ellen Russell Emerson, *Indian Myths*, Boston, 1884, wherein Pidgeon is quoted.
5. *Legends of the Sioux*, Eastman, New York, 1849. Readers interested in the subject of Indian altars will find descriptions, with coloured plates, in the coming work of Surgeon Washington Matthews, U. S. Army, and in the *Snake dance of the Moquis of Arizona*, by the author.

The Kioways of the Great Plains soaked their buffalo hides in urine to make them soft and flexible.[6]

Bernal Diaz, in his enumeration of the articles for sale in the *"tianguez"* or market-places of Tenochtitlan, uses this expression:

> I must also mention human excrements which were exposed for sale in canoes lying in the canals near this square, which is used for the tanning of leather; for, according to the assurances of the Mexicans, it is impossible to tan well without it.— (Bernal Diaz, *Conquest of Mexico*, London, 1844, vol. 1.)

The same use of ordure in tanning bear-skins can be found among the nomadic Apaches of Arizona, although, preferentially, they use the ordure of the animal itself.

Urine figures as the mordant for fixing the colours of blankets and other woollen fabrics woven by the Navajoes of New Mexico, by the Mokis of Arizona, by the Zunis and other Pueblos of the Southwest, by the Araucanians of Chile, by Mexicans, Peruvians, by some of the tribes of Afghanistan, and other nations; by all of whom it is carefully preserved.

> In the valley of Cuzco, Peru, and, indeed, in almost all parts of the Sierra, they used human manure for the maize crops, because they said it was the best. (Garcillasso de la Vega, *Comentarios Reales*, Clement C. Markham's *Translation, in Hakluyt Society*, vol. 45.)

The employment of different manures as fuel for firing pottery among Mokis, Zunis, and other Pueblos, and for general heating in Thibet, has been pointed out by the author in a former work. (*Snake Dance of the Mokis*, London, 1884; New York, 1884.) The dung of the buffalo served the same purpose in the domestic economy of the Plains Indians. (McClintock and Strong, 'Dung. See, also, Kitto's *Biblical Encyclopaedia*, article "Dung.")

Sahagun gives, in detail, the formula of the preparation applied by the Mexicans for the eradication of dandruff:

> Cut the hair close to root, wash head well with urine, and afterward take *amole* (soap-weed) and *coixochitl* leaves—the *amole* is the wormwood of this country [in this Sahagun is mistaken]—

---

6. The whole process was carefully observed by Captain Robert G. Carter, 4th Cavalry, U. S. Army.

117

and then the kernels of *aguacate* ground up and mixed with the ashes already spoken of (wood ashes from the fireplace), and then rub on black mud with a quantity of the bark mentioned [*mesquite*]!

A similar method of dressing the hair, but without urine, prevails among the Indians along the Rio Colorado and in Sonora, Mexico. First, an application is made of a mixture of river mud ("blue mud," as it is called in Arizona) and pounded *mesquite* bark. After three days this is removed, and the hair thoroughly washed with water in which the saponaceous roots of the *amole* have been steeped. The hair is dyed a rich blue-black, and remains soft, smooth, and glossy.

In the examples just given, as well as in a few to follow, where urine is applied in bodily ablutions, the object sought is undoubtedly the procuring of ammonia by oxidation; to none of these can any association of religious ideas be ascribed. Such will not be the case, however, where the ablutions are attended with ceremonial observances, are incorporated in a ritual, or take place in chambers reserved for sacred purposes. No difficulty is experienced in assigning to their proper categories the urinal ablutions of the Eskimo of Greenland, of Alaska, of the northwest coast of America, of the Indians of Cape Flattery, of the people of Iceland, and of the savages of Lower California, or of the Celtiberii of Spain.

> Although they boasted of cleanliness, both in their nourishment and in their dress, it was not unusual for them to wash their teeth and bodies in urine—a custom which they considered favourable to health.—(Maltebrun, *Universal Geography*, article, "Spain," vol. 5, book 137, American edition, Philadelphia, 1832.)

> Pericuis of Lower California, "Mothers, to protect them against the weather, cover the entire bodies of their children with a varnish of coal and urine."—(Bancroft, *idem*, vol. 1.)

> Clavigero not only tells all that Bancroft does, but he adds that the women of California washed their own faces in urine.—(*Historia de Baja California, Mexico, 1852.*)

Ordure in Smoking

Among all the observances of the every-day life of the American aborigines, none is so distinctly complicated with the religious idea as smoking; therefore, should the use of excrement, human or animal, be detected in this connection, full play should be given to the suspicion that a hidden meaning attaches to the ceremony. This would appear to be the view entertained by the indefatigable missionary, De Smet, who records such a custom among the Flatheads and Crows in 1846:

> To render the odour of the pacific incense agreeable to their gods it is necessary that the tobacco and the herb (*skwiltz*), the usual ingredients, should be mixed with a small quantity of buffalo dung.—Father De Smet, *Oregon Missions*, New York, 1847.

The Sioux, Cheyennes, Arapahoes, and others of the plains tribes, to whom the buffalo is a god, have the same or an almost similar custom.

ORDURE AND URINE IN MEDICINE

The administration of urine as a curative opens the door to a flood of thought. Medicine, both in theory and practice, even among nations of the highest development and refinement, has not, until within the present century, cleared its skirts of the superstitious hand-prints of the dark ages. With tribes of a lower degree of culture it is still subordinate to the incantations and exorcisms of the "medicine man."

It might not be going a step too far to assert that the science of therapeutics, pure and simple, has not yet taken form among savages; but to shorten discussion and avoid controversy, it will be assumed here that such a science does exist, but in an extremely rude and embryotic state; and to this can be referred all examples of the introduction of urine or ordure in the *materia medica*, where the aid of the "medicine man" does not seem to have been invoked, as in the method employed for the eradication of dandruff by Mexicans, Eskimo, and others, the Celtiberian dentrifice, &c.

The Indians of California gave urine to newly-born children.

> At time of childbirth many singular observances obtained; for instance, the old women washed the child as soon as it was born and drank of the water; the unhappy infant was forced to take a draught of urine, medicinally.—Bancroft, H. H. *Native Races*, vol. 1.

Padre Inamma, whose interesting researches upon rattlesnake bites and their remedies (made in Lower California, some time before the expulsion of the Jesuits, in 1767) are published in Clavigero, says that the most usual and most efficacious antidote was human ordure, fresh and dissolved in water, drunk by the person bitten.

Occult Influences Ascribed to Ordure and Urine

In Canada, human urine was drunk as a medicine. Father Sagard witnessed a dance of the Hurons in which the young men, women, and girls danced naked around a sick woman, into whose mouth one of the young often urinated, she swallowing the disgusting draught in the hope of being cured.

Urine Used to Defeat Witchcraft

Father Le Jeune must have been on the track of something corresponding to an ur-orgie among the Hurons when he learned that the devil imposed upon the sick, in dreams, the duty of wallowing in ordure if they hoped for restoration to health.

Ordure in Love-Philtres.

The witches and wizards of the Apache tribe make a confection or philtre one of the ingredients of which is generally human ordure, as the author learned from some of them a few years since. The Navajoes, of same blood and language as the Apaches, employ the dung of cows (as related in the *Snake Dance of the Mokis.*).

Burlesque Survivals

The Apaches and Navajoes, close neighbours of the Zunis, have had, until very recently, (as at time of first publication), the Dance of the Joshkân, in which clowns scatter upon the spectators, from bladders wound round their bodies, water, said to be representative of urine.

In the report of one of the early American explorations to the Trans-Missouri region occurs the story that the Republican Pawnees, Nebraska, once (about 1780-'90) violated the laws of hospitality by seizing a calumet-bearer of the Omahas who had entered their village, and, among other indignities, making him "drink urine mixed with bison gall." [7]

Bison gall itself sprinkled upon raw liver, just warm from the carcass, was regarded as a delicacy. The expression "excrement eater" is applied by the Mandans and others on the Upper Missouri as a term of the vilest opprobrium, according to Surgeon Washington Matthews,[8]

---

7. Long's *Expedition, Philadelphia*, 1823, vol. 1.
8. Author of *Hidatsa*, and other ethnological works of authority.

U. S. Army, whose remarks are based upon an unusually extended and intelligent experience.

CONCLUDING REMARKS

MEDICINAL EFFECTS OF URINE.

The only discovery has been in the work of Surgeon General Hammond, U. S. Army.[9] A chapter is devoted to uraemic intoxication or the exhilaration produced by the entrance into the blood of urine, either injected or abnormally absorbed. This part of the subject should be carefully scrutinized by medical experts, whose determinations may make known whether or not the drunken frenzy of the Zuni dancers could be attributed to the unnatural beverage exclusively or to that in combination with other intoxicants.

> Human urine was at one time considered aperient; and was given in jaundice in the dose of one or two ounces. Cow's urine, *urina vaccae.* all-flower water, was once used warm from the cow as a purge.—(Dunglison's *Medical Dictionary,* Philadelphia, Pa., 1860, article "Urine.")

Only such matter has been admitted into this monograph as could *prima facie* be considered as having the right of entry; the greatest care has been taken to avoid distortion or mutilation of authorities, and much has been excluded that might have been presented without running a risk of being accused of unfairness.

For example, as old an authority as John de Laet calls attention to the great prevalence of intoxication and debauchery among the Indians of Vextipa, near Mexico, who on feast days had the ancient custom of becoming drunk as beasts and committing enormous excesses.[10] And in like manner the first missionaries in Canada complained of the brutal orgies of the natives, in which, under cover of darkness and the cloak of their superstitions, deeds were committed which the pen dared not describe. Ample reference to these has been preserved in the Jesuit relations, and in the exact and interesting American treatises dependent so largely upon them.[11] It is more likely, however, that the Huron and Algonkin saturnalia were, in general terms, scenes of promiscuous licentiousness.

---

9. *Physiological Memoirs*, New York, 1863.
10. John de Laet, *lib.* vi, chap, vii.
11. See Francis Parkman's *Jesuits in North America*, the works of John Gilmary Shea, and Kipp's *Jesuit Missions*.

The Snake-Dance of the Moquis

A whirring sound resembling that of rain, driven by summer gusts, issued from the arcade; with this came the clanking of rattles and gourds filled with corn. The dancers were moving down towards us.

First came a barefooted old man, crowned with a garland of cottonwood leaves, holding in his hands in front of him a flat earthen bowl, from which he sprinkled water upon the ground, very much as a Catholic priest would asperse his congregation.[1]

The second old man carried a flat basket of fine corn-meal.

The third held his left hand up to a necklace of bears' claws, while with his right he gently rattled an instrument shaped thus, **T**, painted white.[2]

The next five men were armed with the same odd-looking rattles, but as they marched close behind one another in single file they were not considered as holding the same rank or as discharging functions of an importance equal to those of the old men who advanced alone.

Numbers 9 to 17 inclusive were little boys, from four to seven years old, marching in single file, each bearing one of the **T** shaped rattles.

An interval of five paces separated them from the grown men who had preceded them, and a like distance intervened between them and an old man who bore aloft in his left hand a bow (one of those so gayly ornamented with feathers and horse-hair which had been noticed upon the upper end of the *Estufa* ladders.

With his right hand this old man rapidly twirled a wooden sling, which emitted the shrill rumble of falling rain so plainly heard as the head of the procession was emerging from the arcade.[3]

---

1 See Plate 1.

2. See Plate 2.

3. See Plate 3.

This was the first division of the dance.

The second and last was composed of forty-eight persons, two of them children, and all males; each bore wands of eagle feathers in both hands. The last man of this division bore a bow, the counterpart of that carried by the sling-twirler of the first division.

All the dancers wore, tied to the right knee, rattles made of tortoise-shells and sheep or goat toes, which clanked dismally whenever the leg or body moved. Small bunches of red feathers were attached to the crown of the head, their long black hair hung loose down their backs, their faces were blackened from brow to upper lip, while mouth, lower lip, and chin looked ghastly by contrast with the kaolin daubed over them. Collars of the white sea-shell beads of their own manufacture hung round their necks, and nearly all wore abalone shells glistening on their breasts. Sashes of sea-shell beads covered their bodies from the right shoulder to the left hip.

Their bodies, legs, and arms were naked and greenish-black, without mark or design. Kilts of painted cotton cloth[4] hung from waist to knee, and dangling down to the heels in rear were skins of the fox and coyote.[5] Red buckskin fringe hung from the waist in most cases; and in others, again, cotton-ball pendants ornamented the girdles. The feet were covered with red buckskin *moccasins*, fringed at ankles, and broad white armlets encircled the elbows.

Each division marched solemnly around the sacred stone and between it and the sacred lodge and tree, the first division completing this formula shortly before the second.

The first division aligned itself with back to houses, but quite close to them, and with its right abutting against the lodge and tree.

The old "medicine man," or priest, whom for the sake of convenience we have called No. 1, stood in front of and facing the lodge, holding well before him the platter of water and eagle-feather wand.

When the second division had finished its tour it formed in two ranks facing the first division, and not more than four paces from it. When this alignment was perfected the men and boys of the first division shook their rattles gently, making the music of pattering showers. This movement was accompanied by the men of the second division who waved their eagle-feathers from right to left in accord with the shaking of the rattles.

---

4. See Plate 2

5. The Totonic priests of Ceuteotl (Ceres) were always dressed in the skins of foxes or coyotes—Bancroft, H. H., vol. ii. .

PLATE 1

MEDICINE MAN WITH BOWL OF SACRED WATER

PLATE 2

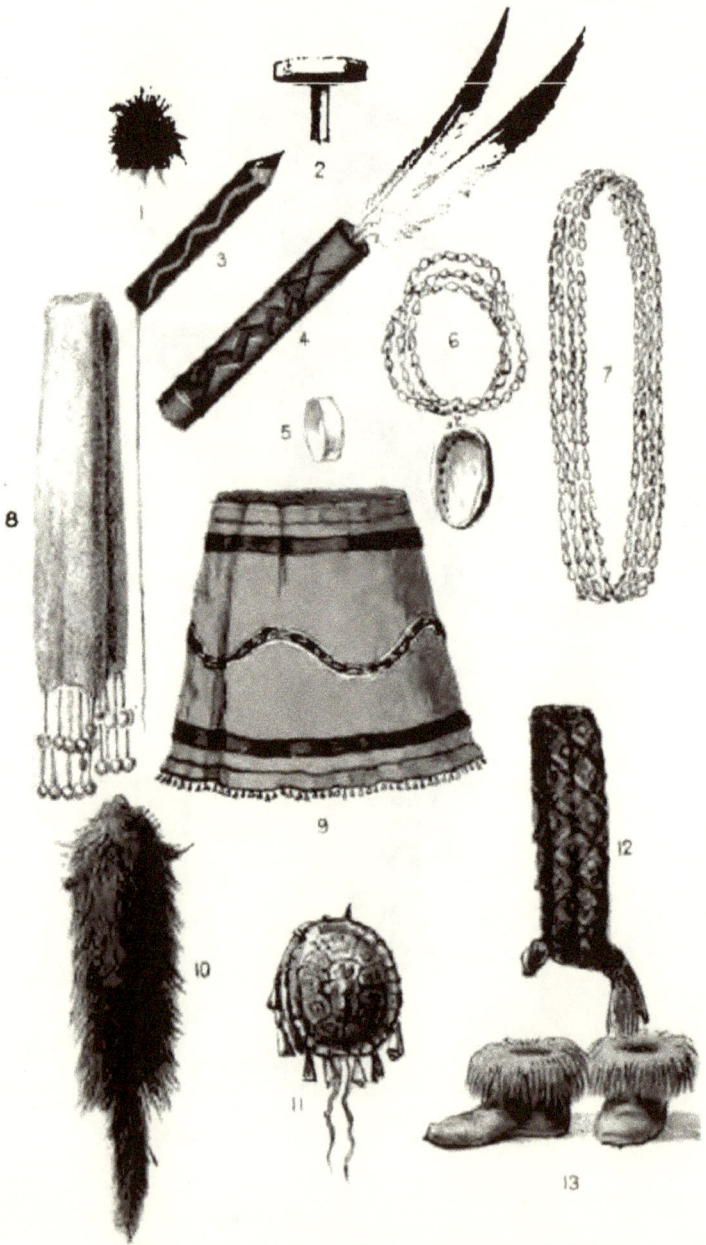

PARAPHERNALIA OF SNAKE DANCERS

PLATE 3

MEDICINE MAN WITH SLING AND MEDICINE BOW

This was repeated eight or ten times, all singing a refrain, keeping time by stamping vigorously with the right foot: "*Oh-ye-haw, oh-ye-haw, ha-yee-ha-ha-yee-ha-ha-yi-ha-a-a-a,*" chanted a dozen times or more with a slow measure and graceful cadence.

This part of the ceremony over, the old man in front of the cottonwood tree and lodge began to pray in a well-modulated and perfectly distinct voice, and sprinkled the ground in front of him with more water, while the second medicine man scattered corn-meal from the platter he was bearing.

Excepting the water–sprinkler[6] (No. 1) and the sling-twirler (No 3), all the first party wore red plumes in hair, red *moccasins*, and white cotton kilts; and their bodies, as already stated, were naked and greenish-black.

The first division remained in place, while the second, two by two, arm in arm, slowly *pranced* around the sacred rock, going through the motions of planting corn to the music of a monotonous dirge chanted by the first division.

A detachment of twenty squaws, maids and matrons, clad in rich white and scarlet mantles[7] of cotton and wool, now appeared, provided with flat baskets and platters, from which they scattered corn-meal in every direction.

This ended the first act.[8]

The first division remained, aligned upon the sacred rock, the head priest (No. 1) intoning a long and fervent prayer, while the second division quietly filed off, going through the arcade. The interlude was very brief. The second division re-emerged from under the arcade, marching two and two as before; but in this section of the programme the left hand files carried snakes in their hands and mouths. The first five or six held them in their hands with the heads of the reptiles to the rights. As the procession pranced closer and closer to where we were seated we saw that the dancers farther to the rear of the column were holding the slimy, wriggling serpents *between their teeth!* The head of the animal in this case also was held towards the right, the object of this being very manifest. The Indians in the right file of the column still retained the eagle wands which their comrades had discarded. With these wands they tickled the heads, necks, and jaws of the snakes, thus distracting, their attention from the dancers in whose teeth they

6. See Plate 1.
7. See Plate 4.
8. See Plates 5 and 6.

were grasped so firmly.

The spectacle was an astonishing one, and one felt at once bewildered and horrified at this long column of weird figures, naked in all excepting the snake painted cotton kilts and red buckskin, *moccasins*; bodies a dark greenish-brown, relieved only by the broad white armlets and the bright yellowish-gray of the fox skins dangling behind them; long elfin locks brushed straight back from the head, tufted with scarlet parrot or woodpecker feathers; faces painted black, as with a mask of charcoal, from brow to upper lip, where the ghastly white of kaolin began, and continued down over chin and neck; the crowning point being the deadly reptiles borne in mouth and band, which imparted to the drama the lurid tinge of a nightmare.

With rattles clanking at knees, hands clinched, and elbows bent, the procession pranced slowly around the rectangle, the dancers lifting each knee slowly to the height of the waist, and then planting the foot firmly upon the ground before lifting the other, the snakes all the while writhing and squirming to free themselves from restraint.

When the snake-carriers reached the eastern end of the rectangle they spat the snakes out upon the ground and moved on to the front of the sacred lodge, tree, and rock, where they stamped strongly with the left foot twice, at same time emitting a strange cry, half grunt and half wail.

The women scattering the corn-meal now developed their line more fully, a portion occupying the terrace directly above the arcade, two or three standing on ladders near the archway, the main body massing in the space between the sacred rock and the sacred lodge, and two or three, reinforced by a squad of devout old crones, doing effective work at the eastern line of the rectangle. Nearly all carried the beautiful, closely-woven, flat baskets, in red, yellow, and black, ornamented with the butterfly, thunder bird, or deer. These baskets were heaped high with finely-ground corn-flour, which was scattered with reckless profusion, not, as previously, upon the ground, but in the air and upon the reptiles as fast as thrown down.

This corn-meal had sacred significance, which it might be well to bear in mind in order to thoroughly appreciate the religious import of this drama. Every time the squaws scattered it their lips could be detected moving in prayer.

In the religious exercises of the neighbouring Indians, the Zunis, the air is fairly whitened with the handfuls of the "*Cunque*," as they call it, flung upon the idols, priests, and sacred flute-players. In all the

PLATE 4

YOUNG GIRL THROWING CORN-MEAL UPON SNAKES

PLATE 5

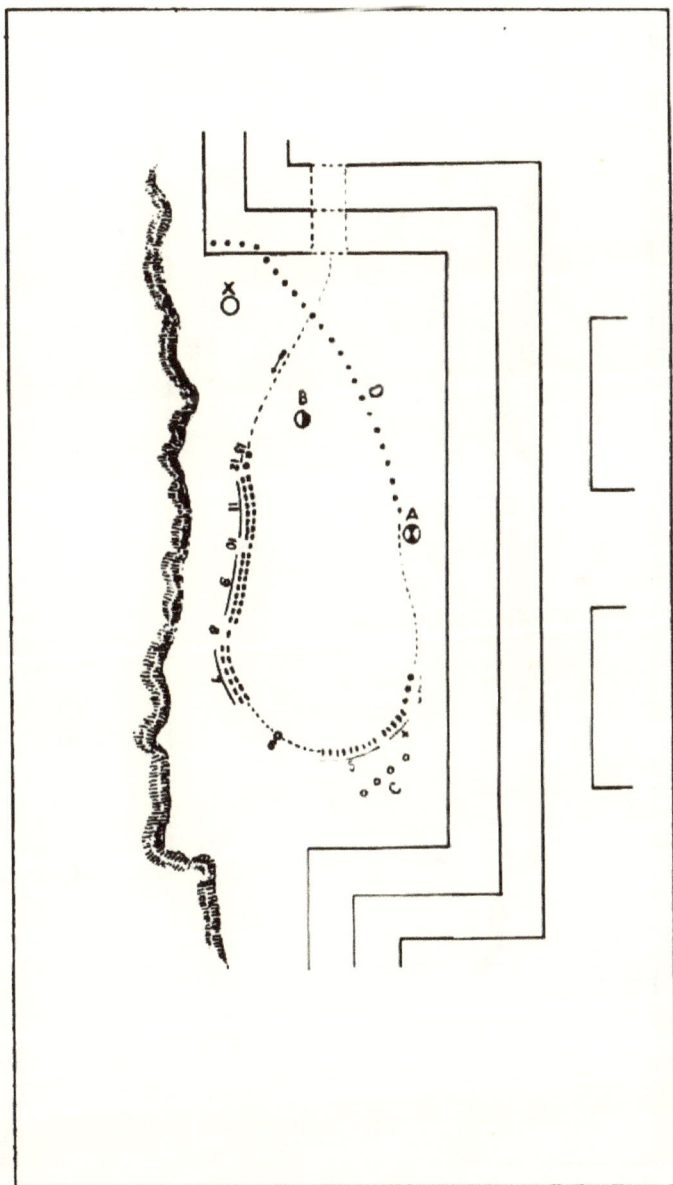

DIAGRAM OF PART I.
A SACRED LODGE, B, SACRED ROCK, C & D. SQUAWS, I, HIGH PRIEST,
2 & 3, MEDICINE MEN, 4; FIVE MEDICINE MEN WITH T SHAPED RATTLES.
5, NINE CHILDREN DITTO, 6, OLD MAN WITH WHISTLING SLING, 7, 8, 9,
AND II, BANDS OF DANCERS, 12 & 13, OLD MEN WITH BOWS, X, ESTUFA.

PLATE 6

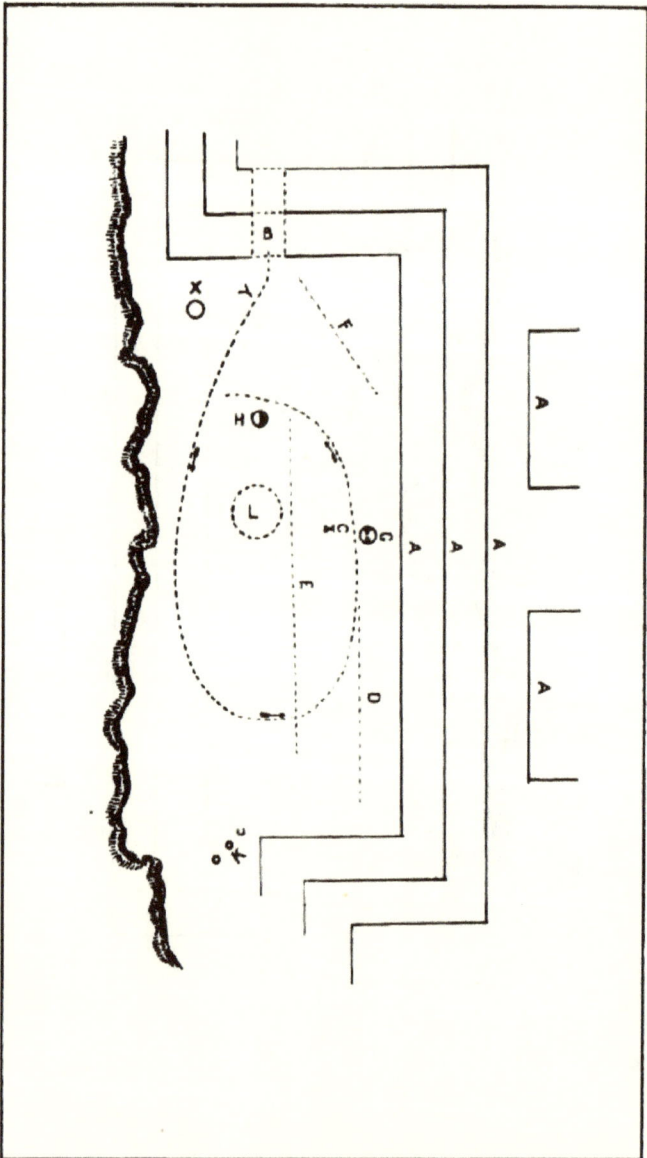

DIAGRAM OF PART 2.
AAAAA, LINE OF HOUSES, B, ARCADE, C, HIGH PRIEST, D, LINE OF
CHORISTERS, E, OF DANCERS, F, OF SQUAWS THROWING MEAL, G, SACRED
LODGE, H, SACRED ROCK, K, SQUAWS THROWING MEAL, L, SACRED CORN RING,
M, EDGE OF PRECIPICE, N N N GOAT AND SHEEP CORRALS, Y, LINE OF
MARCH, INDICATED BY ARROW, X, ESTUFA.

Pueblos along the Rio Grande, or near it, the same farinaceous mixture (since it is generally a mixture of corn-meal, pounded *chalchihuitl*, and other ingredients is offered as a morning sacrifice to the god of day. Go into any house in Jemez, Zia, Santana, San Felipe Acoma, or Zuni, and you will find in a convenient niche a small bowl or basket filled with it to allow each person in the family to throw a small pinch to the east upon rising in the morning. The Zunis and Moquis are never without it, and carry it in little bags of buckskin tied to their waist-belts.

The use of this sacred meal closely resembles the crithmomancy of the ancient Greeks, but is not identical with it. Crithomancy was a divination, by throwing flour or meal upon sacred animals, or upon their viscera after they had been sacrificed; the forms or letters assumed by the meal gave to the soothsayer the clue to the future of which he was in quest. While the Greek priest scattered meal upon the sacred victims, it goes without argument that he prayed, and up to this point the resemblance is perfect; beyond this it would be rash to say that any parallelism exists. The Moquis do not attempt to foretell the future by this means, or at least if they do, my researches have been misleading.[9]

After a snake had been properly sprinkled it was picked up, generally by one of the eagle-wand bearers, but never by a woman, and carried up to the Indians of the first division, which, as was remarked, had preserved its alignment near the sacred lodge. Most of the snakes were transferred to the infant grasp of the little boys who had come in with the first division. One five-year old youngster, in the fearlessness of infancy, stoutly and bravely upheld the five-foot monster which, earlier in the day, had so nearly scared me out of my senses.

This part of the ceremony lasted scarcely a moment; the serpents were at once taken away from the boys and handed to the first old man, whom we have learned to regard and designate as the head priest; and by him, with half-audible ejaculations, consigned to the sanctuary of the sacred lodge.

From this the reptiles made no attempt to escape the hairy coating of the buffalo skin which lined it, keeping them from crawling upward or outward. As fast as the members of the second division had dropped the first invoice of snakes they returned with more, repeating precisely the same ceremony following their first entrance, the only discrepancy

---

9. The Moquis cast corn-meal under the feet of the horses of the Spaniards who visited them in 1692. See Davis' *Conquest of New Mexico*.

being that in their subsequent appearances *every* man carried a sinuous, clammy reptile between his teeth; one of the performers, ambitious to excel his fellows, carried two; while another struggled with a huge serpent too large to be pressed between his teeth, which could seize and retain a small fragment of the skin only, the reptile meanwhile flopping lazily, but not more than half-contentedly, in the air.

The devotion of the bystanders was roused to the highest pitch; maidens and matrons redoubled their energy, sprinkling meal not only upon the serpents wriggling at their feet, but throwing handfuls into the faces of the men carrying them. The air was misty with flour, and the space in front of the squaws white as with driven snow.

Again and again the weird procession circled around the sacred rock. Other dancers, determined to surpass the ambitious young men whose achievements have just been chronicled, inserted two snakes in their mouths instead of one, the reptiles in these cases being, of course, of small size. I must repeat that no steps had been taken to render these snakes innocuous either by the extraction of their fangs or by drugs, and that if they are quiescent while between the teeth of the dancers, it was as much because their attention was distracted by the feather-wands plied so skilfully by the attendants, as from any "medicine" with which they had been bathed or fed; that as soon as they struck the ground, most of them began to wriggle actively and coil up, to the great consternation of the spectators in closest proximity, and that when so moving, the attendants first sprinkled them with corn-meal and then began to tickle them with the eagle-wands to make them squirm out at full length, when they would pounce upon them behind the head, and carry them, held in this secure manner, to the little boys who, grasping them in the same way, seemed to have no apprehensions of danger.

Once or twice snakes of unusual activity had coiled themselves up in attitudes of hostility, from which they were driven, not by the ordinary eagle-wand-bearing attendants, but by older and more dexterous manipulators, whom it is fair to assume were expert charmers. This impression, or assumption, will be strengthened by instances to be recorded later on in the drama.

Two or three serpents struck viciously at all who approached them; one quickly wriggled his way in among the men packed on the outer line of the rectangle, at the crest of the precipice, and another one darted like lightning into the midst of a group of women corn-throwers, raising, especially in the latter case, a fearful hubbub, and creating

Sacred Lodge

ATTENDANT FANNING SNAKES

DANCER HOLDING SNAKE IN MOUTH

a stampede, checked only by the prompt action of the charmers, who, without delay, secured the rebellious fugitives and bore them off in triumph, to be deposited in the buffalo skin sanctuary. After the snakes had all been carried in the mouths of dancers, dropped on the ground, sprinkled with sacred corn-meal, picked up, held by the small boys, passed to the chief priest, and by him been prayed over and deposited in the buffalo lodge or sanctuary, a circle was formed on the ground in front of the sacred rock by tracing with corn-meal a periphery of 20 feet diameter.

The snakes were rapidly passed out from the sanctuary and placed within this circle, where they were completely covered up with sacred meal, and allowed to remain, while the chief priest recited in a low voice a brief prayer.

The Indians of the second division then grasped them convulsively in great handfuls, and ran with might and main to the eastern crest of the precipice, and then darted like frightened hares down the trails leading to the foot, where they released the reptiles to the four quarters of the globe.

While they were running away with the snakes, the first division moved twice around the sacred rock and buffalo lodge, the old man armed with the sling, twirling it vigorously, causing it to emit the same peculiar sound of rain driven by the wind which had been heard on their approach. In passing in front of the sacred rock the second time each stamped the ground with his right foot.

The whole dance did not occupy more than one-half or three-quarters of an hour. The number of snakes used was more than one hundred; the dancers ran backwards and forwards so confusedly that it was not possible to determine certainly how many times the whole division had changed snakes, but it must have been not less than four, and more probably as many as five times.

The opinions of the American bystanders varied as to whether or not any of the dancers were bitten. None were so reported by the Indians, and the proper view to take of this matter must be that while all, or nearly all, the snakes used were venomous, the knowledge and prudence of those handling them averted all danger.

Williams and Webber said that while the dancers were gathering up the snakes to convey them from the sanctuary or buffalo lodge to the circle of corn-meal in the last act one man held *ten* and another *seven*.

After freeing the reptiles at the foot of the *mesa* the men of the second division ran back, breathless and agitated, to their homes.

This was the Snake-Dance of the Moquis, a tribe of people living within our own boundaries, less than seventy miles from the Atlantic and Pacific Railroad in the year of our Lord 1881.

The Tablet Dance of Pueblo

A bridal party knelt at the chancel rails. The bride and groom, as well as the attendants, being in their best raiment, and having their coarse shining hair freshly brushed and banged square across the eyebrows.

The young married couple (for such they already were, the nuptial benediction having been pronounced before mass) were tied together by the priest's stole passing loosely around their necks, and each held in the right hand a burning candle. The bride was attended by a maiden friend who knelt at her left, and the groom by his best man who knelt on his right; while to the right of the whole party, and also on their knees, were the aged, snowy-haired parents of the two young people whom the blessing of the church had just made one.

The Navajo rugs upon which these eight persons knelt were of the most beautiful description.

To the music of an orchestra of cracked fiddles, squeaky guitars, bell, drums, and rusty shot-guns, and of voices cracked worse than the fiddles or guitars, the new statue of Saint Dominick was carried in solemn procession through the streets, which were now a surging mass of Indians from all the neighbouring *pueblos*, Mexicans from as far north as Santa Fé and as far south as Albuquerque, and Americans from the mining districts close by.

Slowly the procession made its way, chanting with an extremely nasal intonation the litany of the saints. In front of the statue was carried a little plaster cast of a dog, from whose mouth projected a flaming torch. This recalled the dream of the mother of Saint Dominick, who, shortly before his birth, imagined that she was to bring into the world a dog as herein depicted. Her fears were soothed by the interpretation that she was to bear a son who should be eloquent and bold as a barking dog, and the fire of whose words should spread a conflagration throughout the universe.

After the congregation had begun to leave the church the bridal party entered the chancel, advanced to the altar, knelt and kissed it reverently, kissed the copy of the Gospels, and then passed completely round behind the altar, the men going by the right and the women by the left, and reuniting in front, when they marched down the nave to the main door, and there turning together, made a profound obeisance back towards the sanctuary. As soon as they had emerged from the building the bride fell behind and followed docilely in the footsteps of her liege lord, who paid no further attention to her.

Padre Ribera told me that the newly-married pair would some time during the day give to all their friends a grand feast, part of which had already been sent over to his house for his breakfast after mass.

He ended his remarks by cordially inviting Moran and myself to eat with him and judge for ourselves what the cooking was like, an invitation promptly and gladly accepted.

The procession made a very complete circuit of both the old and the new *pueblos*, neglecting no street or avenue, until it reached the booth prepared for the reception of the statue early in the day, and which was now gorgeous and fairly ablaze with the dazzling colours of the choicest productions of the Navajo looms.

The procession having deposited the statue of Saint Dominick in its niche, abruptly dissolved, a few only of the more zealous and devout remaining on their knees to implore the advocacy of their patron for some desired object. Most of the men, women, and children hurried to their homes to dress or undress for the dance, the main feature of the day's work.

Clowns were already running about from house to house, giving warning to those who were to enact parts of any prominence.

We now took another glance through the small rectangular windows on the ground-floor of the *Estufas*.

Each was almost full of young men, women, and children. The men were nearly naked, their bodies painted white, hair done up at the sides in horns, wound with corn-shucks; bands of cedar sprigs encircled their bodies from shoulders to waist, and rattles of tortoise-shells and sheep's toes were pendent from the rear of right knee. A number of old men were haranguing them, but upon what topic I could not discover.

All—old and young, and of both sexes—wore curious head-dresses of thin boards, painted pea-green and sky blue, with tips of red or yellow, and with incisions in shape of the crescent, cross, square, or letter **T**.

Small white flecks of eagle-down floated from the corners of those worn by the squaws.[1]

The garments worn by the women were the same as those in general use among those of the Zunis and Moquis, that is, a single garment, woven of dark blue wool, reaching to the knees. The left arm and shoulder and the upper half of left breast were exposed, and the right arm almost so. But the Santo Domingo women wore, under these, clean white petticoats with ruffled and scalloped edges, which were allowed to project an inch below the woollen skirts, producing a very pretty effect. Their long hair, smooth and polished as jet, was carefully brushed over their shoulders and down their backs.

They were all barefooted and barelegged, but so neat and clean was each and every one that I can say never before or since have I seen so pleasing an assemblage of what might in all fairness claim the title of savage beauty.

The men were arrayed uniformly with regard to the kilt of white cotton cloth, made by the Zunis and Moquis, and evidently preserved in the same family for generations.

Each dancer of either sex carried a little sprig of cedar in the left hand.[2]

Just as we passed they began to sally out from the *Estufas*. Down the stairs filed an even hundred, not counting the standard-bearer, but including a chorus of a dozen men, who worked themselves into a frenzy, keeping time to the thump, thump, thumping of an oblong, keg-shaped drum, made of a hollow cottonwood log, covered with skin, the body of the instrument being yellow and the "trimmings" blue.

For a long time I found it impossible to catch the refrain, but by persistent effort I at last made out the concluding words of each verse,

"*Wi-ka-tolli-ná-mashé-é-é-é-é;*"

which were repeated over and over again in excellent time and with increasing vehemence.

While the dancers were arranging themselves in proper order we

---

1. For Head-dress, see Plate 1.
2. See Plates 2., 3., and 4.

had plenty of time to hunt up Padre Ribera and sample his breakfast.

We were welcomed with cordiality, and introduced to all the cooks and attendants. To frame an opinion from what I saw that morning Padre Ribera must be held in high repute by his flock.

Three young girls had been detailed to cook, wash the dishes, and set the table; as many old women chaperoned, superintended, bustled about, and made themselves general nuisances, under the impression that they were rendering invaluable service; and half a dozen old men, more or less lazy and decrepit, did what might be called "the heavy standing around."

The young girls were models of neatness, modesty, and decorum; their hands and faces were clean as amber; their hair freshly washed with "*aurole*," brushed and tied up; their dresses new and bright, under each the crisply starched petticoat and a cotton chemise covering arms, neck, and bosom.

While cooking, washing dishes, or setting table, they wore white cotton cloths tied round the neck and covering the dress in front.

The *padre* invited us to be seated, and then gave the signal to bring in the repast. A big Indian grabbed in one hand a saddle of mutton roasted over the coals and cut it into large "gobs," any one of which would have been plenty for a small family.

To each guest one of these was handed by the attendants, who accompanied it with a correspondingly great hunch of bread and a bowl of rich goat's milk.

The centre of the table was reserved for a pile of melons and two platters, one containing boiled, the other fried, eggs. During the meal there was the greatest confusion; Indians kept running in or out, on business or pleasure intent. The business was largely comprehended in falling over each other's feet and over a pack of mangy curs which the appetising odours of the roast meat had attracted inside the house; while the pleasure seemed to consist in scratching their heads, or in gazing at the strangers with open mouths and open eyes.

There was enough confusion to drive a saint mad. Padre Ribera, however, never lost his good-humour, and indeed infected us with a fair portion of his own joviality.

"Captain," he said, turning to me, "did you ever know that in olden times the Spanish priests who lived among these Indians used to keep journals of their daily lives, in which were narrated all that the Indians had done or said? It would be a great thing for you to get some of those journals, would it not?"

PLATE 1

1, SACRED STANDARD. 2 HEAD DRESSES
3 BORDER OF STANDARD. 4 DRUM.

PLATE 2

FEMALE DANCER, DANCE OF THE TABLET,
PUEBLO OF SANTO DOMINCO, NEW MEXICO

PLATE 3

MALE DANCER, DANCE OF THE TABLET,
PUEBLO OF SANTO DOMINCO, NEW MEXICO

PLATE 4

CLOWN DANCER, DANCE OF THE TABLET,
PUEBLO OF SANTO DOMINCO, NEW MEXICO

"Yes, Father Ribera, I appreciate fully the wonderful labours of those devoted men, and I regret extremely that some plan cannot be devised by our Government, or by private associations interested in the early history of our country, to get back those books, or copies of them, from the city of Mexico, Simancas in Spain, or wherever else they may be stored. I think they would be almost priceless."

Our conversation was here broken off abruptly by the sound of the approaching procession, and sallying out, we took our places in the shade of the church to see it pass. The first division of the dance was now moving slowly and sedately into the church "*plaza*," the formation being in column of twos, the men on the right, the woman on the left. The men were all bareheaded, hair flowing loose, and with parrot feathers tied to front of crown. They were naked, except that Scotch kilts of white cotton Zuni cloth reached half-way to the knees, the lower edge of the kilts being generally fringed with a narrow border of black. Their bodies were painted a reddish pink with, in occasional instances, streaks of white. This same pinkish white was applied to the legs from knees to ankles, but above the knees and the forearms were a dead white.

Above the elbows were broad green armlets holding sprigs of cedar in place.

Hanging from the rear of the waist-belts were coyote or fox skins, tails downward.[3] No leggings were worn, but around the calves were green, black, or yellow garters, with small shell pendants, which rattled in unison with the music of tortoise backs and sheep's toes tied to the right knee, or of small painted gourds, filled with corn, shaken in the right hand.

These men wore *moccasins* trimmed around the ankles with goats' hair.[4]

The women and girls carried on their heads painted tablets, already mentioned: they were bare-legged, bare-footed, wore no garters or tortoise-shell rattles, and carried no gourds, but each bore a fair-sized bunch of cedar in her left hand.

The necklaces of the women were of hollow silver spheres, strung like rosaries, and having pendant from them double or archiepiscopal crosses of silver.

The departures from this uniformity of decoration were not nu-

---

3. "The Totonac priests of Ceuteotl (Ceres) were always dressed in the skins of foxes or coyotes."—Bancroft, H. H., vol. ii.
4. See Plate 3.

merous, and consisted altogether of necklaces of fine shells, malachite or coral, of home manufacture, bored out by the bow-drill with flint tip, in the use of which the Indians of this *pueblo* are unusually dexterous. I also noticed, as a pendant, a crescent of solid silver, outlining the man in the moon.[5]

The management of this division of the dance was under the care of three or four clowns, who were naked excepting the breech-clout, and wore no *moccasins*; their bodies, limbs, and faces were striped black and white; bands of otter fur crossed their bodies diagonally; tortoise-shells clanked at their right knees, cedar sprigs encircled ankles and waists, and corn-shucks tied up their hair. [6]

With this first hundred were numbers of tiny children not counted in the aggregate.

The step of the dance was a "mark-time," something between a shuffle and a goose step; in advancing slowly the body was bent forward.

Thus the procession worked its way round the *plaza*, the clowns prancing hither and thither, waving small wands of Cottonwood branches.

When in front of the church and Padre Ribera's position, the fun grew fast and furious; the clowns darted hither and thither, bellowing orders; the drummers and choristers gave us another dose of

"*Wi-ka-tolli-ná-mashé-é-é-é-é;*"

while the dancers, now facing each other, but preserving the same step, turned round and round in place for several moments, ending in a series of terpsichorean evolutions, rather too complicated for my descriptive powers, at the termination of which they marched away rapidly in single file, each woman or girl falling in behind her male partner as he passed her, and the orchestra and clowns giving a farewell howl ere they joined their comrades.

The dress of the dancers evidently perpetuated the pre-historic costume of their forefathers. Not a few of the kilts were worn threadbare, although all were clean. There was also to be seen a number of

---

5. This ornament is to be found among the Navajoes, who occasionally make it, and who say that it has some connection with their worship of Ah-sun-nuth, or the Woman in the Western Ocean. While I was among the Navajoes, in April and May 1881, my old friend Mr. Leonard obtained for me, with much difficulty, a couple of these ornaments; one of the pair is at this moment in the private collection of Lieutenant-General P. H. Sheridan, U.S. Army, (as at time of first publication).
6. See Plate 4.

the Moqui and Zuni girdles of cotton, terminating in a string and ball fringe. These are so highly regarded by all the Pueblos that it is a matter of extreme difficulty to obtain one of them.

INDIAN CLOWNS

A brief interlude followed, and then the second division entered the *plaza*, headed by a standard with a border varying only slightly, if at all, from that upon the banner borne by the first division. In advance of this division was borne another oblong drum, with white body, black heads, and red "points." In this division there were twenty-four choristers, eighty dancers, twelve clowns, and twenty-six children. In attire they were almost the counterparts of their respective predecessors, but the bodies, arms, and legs of the male dancers were painted *blue*, and the bodies of the clowns streaked with the same colour. The wooden head-dresses of the women were painted bluish green, tipped on the upper corners with red and yellow, and perforated with crescent or square holes.

The modest deportment of the gentler sex attracted general comment. During the whole dance numbers of them never raised their eyes from the ground. The beauty of the women was in a few cases enhanced, but in most impaired, by patches of vermilion painted on each cheek.

The second division of dancers went through the same evolutions as their comrades of the first, whom they soon followed to the shrine of Santo Domingo, whither Moran and I also proceeded under a broiling sun.

The two bodies of dancers, massed together, made a scene resplendent with gorgeous colouring; the dark blue blanket-skirts of the squaws, girt with red and green worsted sashes; their long, black, glistening hair; the vivid green of the head-dresses, and the darker hues of the cedar sprigs; the dangling feathers of eagle and parrot; the painted legs and arms of the men, or the glistening white petticoats of the women, heightened the barbaric splendours of Navajo blankets and the sheen of silver necklaces.

Each Indian in turn filed into the shrine of Saint Dominick, and presented an offering of a candle, or else the first-fruits of his melon-patch or cornfield,—the donations swelling into a grand pile of loaves of bread, candles, and Apache baskets filled with plums and melons,—all of which the stolid attendants upon the shrine apathetically deposited at one side.

The clowns made the most of the chance now given to display their wit; they approached the shrine with mock obeisance, addressed the saint with simulated humility and deference, affected to hand him their offerings, called him "*Tata*" (father) in a very familiar way, and perpetrated jokes which must have been coeval with the veteran witticisms of the American circus, if the impassive serenity with which the grown men and women received them could be accepted as an indication.

The melons and other presents tendered by the clowns and dancers were handed to them by friends and relatives in waiting as they drew near the statue.

One of the clowns offered a melon to a miner, who accepted it as a *bona fide* gift; but the Indian snatched it out of his hands, and darted away through the crowd to the unrestrained delight of the youngsters, who, it should be said, were giggling heartily at everything said and done for their diversion.

Elbowing my way about in the closely-packed mass of spectators, I had abundant opportunity for seeing all that was prized in the way of personal decoration in Santo Domingo. Nearly every old squaw in the *pueblo* wore one of the silver rosary necklaces already mentioned. It then occurred to me that somewhere I had read that when the Spaniards reconquered New Mexico, in 1692-94, their commanding general, D. Diego Vargas, imposed upon the Rio Grande Pueblos the condition that each full-grown man and woman should habitually wear round the neck a rosary as a mark of subjection to the Crown of Spain and the true Church; and at same time insisted upon the discontinuance of the dance in honour of the idols, called by the Castilians the Cochino or Pig, from its ugly snout, but known among the Zunis, who still practise it as the dances of the Coyamashé or Shalacu.[7]

When the rosary ceased to be a badge of subjection it might have been refined into an ornament, and its use continued long after the tradition of its introduction had faded from the minds of the Indians themselves. The Cochino dance never was openly revived so long as the Spaniards could prevent it; yet it is possible that the Dance of the Tablet may have afforded a satisfactory substitute. And, further, may not these exercises have been a compromise between the prejudices of those who tenaciously clung to the old heathen rites and the incli-

---

7. Consult Davis' *Conquest of New Mexico*. The incident mentioned occurred, but the officer was named Cruzate. He entered New Mexico about 1690. I am confident that Vargas, who came after him in 1692-94, imposed the same badge of subjection.

nations of others whom fear, venality, superior intelligence, or hidden sympathy attracted to the doctrines of the conquerors?

Certain it is that every symbol seen here this day has been seen at other times among the Zunis, Moquis, and Jemez people, with whose heathenism they are linked, and if heathenish in those *pueblos*, they can scarcely be Christian in Santo Domingo.

These remarks apply, of course, only to such of the Indians as have not accepted the teachings of the Spanish missionaries. It must not be forgotten that there is a very respectable percentage seemingly imbued with Christian fervour, and humbly and devoutly following in the footsteps of the Master.

The dancers, after depositing their gifts, resumed their places in line, and continued without intermission, until the sun had sunk to rest, their performances in singing, drumming and shuffling.

The amount of the offerings was considerable; the quality was not very good. It looked to me as if this part of the proceedings was more complimentary than otherwise, since no man in his sound senses would think of eating the immature melons and plums unless he had his life insured at a high figure.

The monotonous drumming and the nasal intonation of the singers grew wearisome after a while, and as there was still much to be seen in the *pueblo* itself, we sauntered leisurely through it, examining everything in a deliberate manner.

One of the first things attracting my attention was a meeting between a pair of lovers; they had evidently only lately had a quarrel, for which each was heartily sorry. He approached, and was received with a disdain tempered with so much sweetness and affection that he wilted at once, and, instead of boldly asserting himself, dared do nothing but timidly touch her hand. The touch, I imagine, was not disagreeable, because the girl's hand was soon firmly held in his, and he with earnest warmth was pouring into her ears words whose purport it was not difficult to conjecture.

It was at this stage of the proceedings that I came upon the scene. They detected my presence, and manifested no particular pleasure at my company; as I did not wish to embarrass them, I at once took my departure.

The young man was unusually good-looking, with a countenance expressive of fine attributes; the maiden was quite pretty, of good figure, and modest, gentle demeanour, and dressed in the full agony of *pueblo* fashion. I hope that by this time they are married and happy.

So much stuff and nonsense have been written about the entire absence of affection from the Indian character, especially in the relations
between the sexes, that it affords me great pleasure to note this little
incident, in which the parties acted with perfect freedom from the
restraint the known presence of strangers imposes. Padre Ribera gives
these people a high character for virtue.

On our return we found that the Lieutenant-Governor had sent
to say that he would like to see us down at our house; as we suspected,
upon the subject of our rent. The room we occupied was the ordinary
apartment of the poorer classes of the country, without furniture of
any kind, and worth, as rents go there, about 25c. a day. The hay, wood,
water, eggs, and everything received had been paid for at prices so
liberal that I suppose the cupidity of our esteemed friend had been
aroused, and he had come to look upon us as a couple of perambu-
lating silver-mines, or perhaps thought that we were Jay Gould and
William H. Vanderbilt out on a picnic.

He began his remarks by blandly expressing his gratification that
the great father in Washington had sent out two of his best men to
give an account of the *pueblo* and the dance; that his heart was very
"content" to have us there, and that he had given us his best room to
sleep in and stay in while we remained in the *pueblo*; and as he had
such a high opinion of the great father and ourselves, he would charge
us only ten dollars for the day. This generosity overwhelmed us. An
abundant charge would have been 50 c.

The Moquis of Arizona

A Brief Description of Their Towns, Their Manners
and Customs

The country of the Moquis Indians, a nation concerning whose manners and origin, no little discussion has been carried on in the Eastern papers during the past year, is situated in the north-eastern portion of Arizona Territory, between the 100th meridian and the Little Colorado River, from east to west, and the Big and Little Colorado Rivers from north to south. The yawning canons through which these rivers force their way. interpose, except at a few widely separated and scarcely known crossing places, impassable barriers to the ingress of strangers, who after encountering successfully this obstacle, find themselves confronted by a desert, seventy-five miles long, upon which for days the weary traveller may wander without having his eyes gladdened by the sight of a single tree, a blade of grass, or a drop of water.

To these frowning canons and to this torrid desert, the Moquis are indebted for the seclusion which has enabled them to preserve intact customs and modes of life derived from the ancient so-called civilization of the Aztecs, with whom their connection may perhaps be established by the recorded fact that in, or about, the year 1536, not much more than a decade and a half after Cortez had overthrown the empire of Montezuma, their towns were first visited by Spanish missionaries, representatives of that class of zealous friars who shortly after the discovery of America, overran the continent, preaching to tribes of Indians, now extinct and forgotten, the merits of the Gospel, whose blessed precepts their own countrymen so persistently disregarded.

Not satisfied with the doctrines, or not relishing the intrusion of the "*padres*," the Moquis condemned some to death and the survivors to ignominious servitude. The Spanish authorities by some means be-

coming apprised of the predicament of the missionaries, speedily or-
ganized for their deliverance an imposing expedition which, under its
leader. Coronado. slowly made its way to the "seven cities of Cibola,"
pictured by Spanish fanaticism as the abode of Satan, and by Spanish
cupidity as the casket of untold treasure. The extrication from a life
of misery of one wretched friar may have rewarded the expedition
for privations endured, and compensated for the treasures it failed to
find: but with its further movements we have nothing to do, except to
mention that upon his return march through the vast regions to the
east ward, Coronado is believed by some writers to have been the first
European who ever saw the buffalo, the wild cattle of the plains.

At long intervals of time, other exploring parties penetrated these
unknown recesses, our own government having had under its patron-
age, the expeditions of Whipple, Beale, Ives, and, lately Wheeler, all
officers of the army or navy, whose published reports are filled with
complete and interesting descriptions of the country. But to the people generally of the United States the Moquis are less known than any
other tribe of Indians within our borders, the few Mormons visiting
them from Utah, or occasional mining parties passing their towns
from the Rio Grande, not being sufficiently numerous to bridge the
chasm of isolation intervening between them and ourselves.

Perched like the castles of German robber-barons, upon the apices
of vertical rocky bluffs, the Moqui towns overlook for miles in every
direction the surrounding country, rendering it an impossibility for
any party whether with hostile or friendly intent to invade the envi-
rons of their settlements without immediate discovery. These bluffs or
"*mesas*" are impregnable to direct assault, and the subjugation of these
people by hostile invasions from the neighbouring tribes, supposing
such ever to be made, would be reduced to a precarious dependence
upon a closely drawn siege, provided against in the ample supplies laid
by each harvest, in their villages.

Seven communities, severed from each other and the outside world,
acknowledge the name of Moquis, but the two languages spoken are
distinct and demand the services of interpreters when communication
is being held among the different villages. A third dialect degenerat-
ing or advancing into a third language, shows how slender a thread of
intercourse holds this nation together, and adds much to the difficulty
of corresponding with them.

Tegua, Hualpi and Moqui ——, occupy the easternmost "*mesa;*"
Oraybe the one farthest to the west, while Su-powa-lery, Su-mo-

powy, and Mu-shang-nevy are built upon a high bluff about midway between the others and a little south of the line connecting them Oraybe makes pretensions to being the principal town; its general dilapidation and thriftless appearance poorly support these claims which may with more justice be conceded to Tegua, Hualpi and Moqui, a description of which will apply equally well to all the others. These three towns nearly cover the flat summit of a *"mesa"* of sand stone, quite 500 feet in vertical height and varying in width from 200 yards to ten feet. Approach is made by climbing a graded way, built up of large blocks of stone, running from summit to base. At every turn, assailants would meet with destruction either by rocks thrown from above or arrows thrown by foemen concealed in inaccessible positions.

The principal passage-way here described is used generally as an easy road for their animals loaded with fuel or the produce of the field. Numerous trails beaten into the vertical face of the precipice having stone steps in the more difficult places, are used in moving quickly from the villages to the springs and reservoirs below. These springs deserve more than a passing notice. Excavated from 25 to 30 feet deep, the Moquis have walled them in with masonry and skilfully constructed ramps leading by a gentle slope to the edge of the water. In each village one spring is reserved for their great herds of black sheep and goats as well as for their *"burros,"* while the other supplies drinking water to the households.

The material used in erecting their dwellings and other edifices is the friable sandstone of their eyrie home; walls, in general, average not more than seven feet in each story, the upper stories receding from the lower until the fourth and last is reached and found to include not more than two or three rooms. Flooring is made of cottonwood rafters, covered with reeds laid on evenly and plastered two or three inches deep with cement, which likewise coats the walls. In some houses a wash, made from the yellow ochreous earth abundant in the vicinity gives a pleasing tone to the interior.

Once on top of the *mesa* the traveller follows along trails worn six and eight inches into the sandstone; boldly pushes his way through a crowd of yelping, vicious, worthless curs, sustains with composure the cynical criticism of patriarchal goats surveying him from sandstone crags or lofty roofs, tramps upon a few lazy chickens, sees scampering before him a horde of dirty, naked children, finds the streets filled with all the garbage and offal of a Hottentot village, inhales all the smells of Cologne and a thousand others Coleridge never knew and finally stands at the foot of a ladder leading to the second floor of one of the buildings.

The ground floor is the kennel inhabited by the dogs and chickens of the family, and sometimes, though not frequently, used as a store-room for corn, melons and peaches, the staple products of the soil.

The Moquis receive visitors customarily with urbanity and are not slow to offer a collation to any who may enter their abodes. If the traveller will now employ his eyes judiciously, much may be observed that is very strange and deserving of recollection. First, the women who had betaken themselves for refuge to the housetops, regaining confidence, cautiously approach the apartment and resume the routine of domestic labour.

Far superior to any other nation in Arizona are the Moquis in matters of dress. The outer garment of the women consists of a dark woollen blanket or gown, fastened by a herring bone stitch of yellow embroidery at the right shoulder and extending down halfway between the knees and ankles; both arms, neck and the upper half of the left breast are exposed; a girdle of red worsted confines the waist, while a line of yellow decoration adorns the dress about six inches below the neck and another the same distance above the lower edge. The hair of the young maidens is arranged in three puffs, one at each side and one at the top of the head, giving a pronounced Mongolian cast to the features.

When in grand costume, the Moqui *belle* dons a necklace of blue and white beads and carefully powders her face with fine corn-meal. The matrons appear much more sedate than the unmarried women and wear their hair in two bands, one lapping over each ear. The men clothe themselves in trousers and shirts of cotton, *moccasins* of deer skin and blankets of home manufacture, in which they envelop the person from head to foot. Great care is taken by both sexes in keeping the head clean and their long tresses glossy and straight. Part of the equipment of every well regulated Moqui family is a bundle of hair brushes of evenly cut hay with which they make their daily toilet.

The children, until well advanced in years, roam about in the Garden of Paradise costume, entirely neglected by their parents and consequently are filthy and repulsive.

While the squaws prepare the daily meal or the refreshment for the visitors, the latter may curiously scrutinize culinary matters and the arrangements of the edifice. In one corner of each room is a small hearth burning a few pieces of cedar wood, brought on the backs of donkeys for a distance of ten or fifteen miles. Over the handful of live coals is fixed a sheet of tin, iron, or stone, now hot enough to serve the purpose of bread baking. Kneeling down before the hearth, the woman stirs up a thin gruel, already prepared in an earthen ware bowl; dipping her hand in the gruel she rapidly spreads the mixture over the heated plate of iron, and the bread almost as rapidly bakes. In appearance it might readily be mistaken for tissue paper, like it, being rolled up in cylindrical bundles and laid aside for future use. This is the favourite bread of the Moquis; but another kind is made from their purple corn-meal, which when presented for use looks like a blue banana. Both varieties are sweet, palatable and nutritious.

The dietary of this people is more comprehensive than, that of any other aboriginal nation now living within the borders of our country. In every building may be seen rooms used as pantries and provision closets, where are kept quantities of red, yellow and blue corn, sometimes hanging on strings, sometimes piled up like cord wood. Watermelons, musk melons, cantaloupes, and peaches of large size and delicious flavour—all these either dried or fresh or both; onions, tomatoes, chili, beets, beans, acorns, sunflower seeds, and "*mescal*" this last obtained by trading with the Apaches. Of the above, corn and melons are planted in extensive fields; hundreds and thousands of acres of cultivated land can be seen at one time, (as at time of first publication).

The peach orchards of all the towns are extensive, but those of Oraybe equal all the others united and produce a larger and more grateful fruit. The Spanish priests brought the first seeds with them. The tomato, onion, and beet are evidently of later introduction, and probably have been obtained from Americans. Sunflowers attain an enormous size, the disks of not a few being more than a foot in diameter; the seeds are esteemed a luxury. "*Mescal*" is obtained by roasting the heart and leaves of the American aloe, a plant that does not grow in the Moqui country, but which furnishes the principal food of the Apaches. Dried mutton, venison, and goats flesh, with an occasional rabbit or hare, comprise the list of meats, while wild honey is sometimes seen as a rare delicacy, preserved in earthen jars.

Meals are served on the cement floor, the men eating first, women and children waiting deferentially until their lords and masters are gorged and then falling to upon the remnants. Beside each guest is placed a roll of tissue bread and in the centre one or two crockery bowls containing a fragrant "*olla podrida*" of chopped mutton, beans, tomatoes, chili and corn. Knives and forks are unknown, so dirty paws

159

dart quickly from dish to mouth, and from mouth to dish until the last fragment of meat has been consumed or satiety compels a respite. Melons and peaches form the after course.

Having satisfied the inner man, there is now an opportunity for looking into the other apartments. In some, buckskin ropes stretched from wall to wall, sustain heavy blankets woven in alternate bands of black, white and blue, the dark colours predominating less generally than the white. Rude weaving machines may be witnessed in operation any time. On the floor are rugs or mats about seven feet long and as many wide, woven of wool, filled in in some way with the fur of coyotes, wolves, rabbits and hares. These cover in cold weather the entrances and windows, as the Moquis have no doors; in summer, these rugs serve as cushions and mattresses. Chimneys are of crockery, and so skilful is their construction, that it is doubtful if a smoking one can be found in "the seven cities." Crockery is indeed the great manufacture of the Moquis whose dishes are not only neat and durable, but ornamented with identically the same tracings as are detected upon the broken fragments of earthenware lying in heaps in the "Aztec ruins" of Arizona.

As might be inferred from the above brief list of comforts possessed by the Moquis, they are a thrifty, frugal and industrious people—one of the few native tribes which do not impose all the drudgery of domestic and outdoor labour upon the women. With them the men assume the care of the fields and nocks, the women employing their time in caring for their homes, weaving blankets, making pottery, and, in the proper season, drying peaches. Squads of five and six women, young and old, assemble in the orchards, gather the delicious fruit and spread it out to dry in the sun; thousands of pounds may be collected within a radius of as many yards.

Every year in the Summer months, detachments of Moquis appear in Prescott, Arizona, the Mormon settlements of lower Utah, and in Santa Fe, New Mexico, to trade for and buy necessaries or any clothing they may fancy. Among frontiersmen, the impression prevails that to them the wild Apache and Navajo have resorted, when at war with the whites, for powder, shot, and rifles. For this belief good grounds exist the Moqui representing the Chatham-street trader of the native American tribes, and disposed to sell all that is most dear to him to secure good bargains. The wilder and nobler Apache and Navajo disdain the effeminate Moqui over whom their superiority must be conceded in every manly and barbaric virtue.

Between Apaches and Moquis the contrast is striking; the former inured to the privations of nomadic life and darkened by constant exposure to the sun; the latter enjoying all comforts attainable by a people ignorant of the working of metals but enervated by an almost monastic seclusion and blanched by the protection of cool and lofty houses. The comparative fairness of the Moqui complexion has given rise to frequent remark, undiminished by encountering among them individuals of pure white skins, auburn hair and ruddy cheeks, corresponding to the Albinos of Equatorial Africa. They say that long ago these Albinos were numerous, but are at present much reduced, probably not over fifty living in the entire nation. The other Moquis do not intermarry with them and the existence of a mutual contempt may be detected, (as at time of first publication).

Little is known of the mode of government or religion prevailing in their villages; the head captains or *caciques*, called in their language "*mung-wee*" transact all business, send out the herds to pasture at day dawn, and recall them to the corrals before sunset; designate the two sentinels who on each "*mesa*" keep watch by night and to all appearances have general supervision of the communities.

A faint flush of religion or superstition tinges their daily life, ushered in each morning by the chanting of choruses and clanging of bells to drive bad spirits away from their harvests and orchards.

Shrines, containing votive offerings of petrified wood, twigs, and other rubbish have been noticed, but thus far no circumstantial account of their festivals, if any, or the ceremonial observed during their continuance, has been compiled. Like all other Indian nations, their traditions, historical and religious, are probably vague, incoherent and unsatisfactory. Much might be gleaned by a careful and intelligent study of the tracings upon the huge blocks of soft, friable sandstone lying about their villages; upon these are carved, not seldom of an enormous size, representations of elk, deer, horses, "*burros*," chickens, crows, men and women; the artists who aspired to the delineation of the human form divine nor being restrained by any considerations of delicacy in the accomplishment of their tasks. Many of these tracings are scarcely discernible and bear marks of a great antiquity.

To the archaeologist and ethnographer this peculiar people of the remote Southwest, must, for a long time to come, furnish matter for reflection and discussion. Their habitations, manners and customs are today practically what they were when Cortez was "Marquis of Oaxaca," 350 years ago; and, if from their condition we may assume, as we have a right to do, a similarity in all respects between them and the other nations of Mexico encountered by the first Spanish adventurers, we must frame new ideas of the Aztecs whose advanced civilization formed the theme of soldiery report and monkish story; the gorgeous palaces of Montezuma fade away and leave us villages of squalid stone tenements; instead of a homogeneous and strongly cemented autonomy, we see a nation composed of many peoples, distrustful each of the other, indifferent to the maintenance of peace at home and impotent to resist aggressions from abroad. Historial iconoclasts have ere this alluded to Montezuma as a petty captain, his capital as a paltry and disorderly jumble of mud huts. The eloquence of Prescott has gilded the achievements of Cortez with the glamour of romance; but the coming generation may applaud the Spanish commander more for what he tried to do than for what he really won.

THE MOQUIS

On the fourth page of the *Alta* today, (as at time of first publication), may be found a very interesting article upon the Moquis of Arizona; that curious people so different from every ether tribe of natives of the country. It is next to impossible to believe they had the same origin as the Apache and other Indian tribes. If they are relics of the old Aztec races, they must have very essentially degenerated, or the Spanish accounts of the Aztec nations, whom they, under Cortez, overcome, were highly coloured. Surely the people who constructed such cities as Palenque must have been at some time in the far past a race vastly advanced beyond the present state of semi-civilization displayed by the Moquis of the present time. But who knows what the effects of their surroundings, their neighbours, the Apaches and other warlike and brutal tribes, may have been. The article referred to is a very interesting account of this strange people, and was written from personal observation and may be implicitly relied upon.

LEONAUR

ALSO FROM LEONAUR
AVAILABLE IN SOFTCOVER OR HARDCOVER WITH DUST JACKET

AN APACHE CAMPAIGN IN THE SIERRA MADRE by *John G. Bourke*—An Account of the Expedition in Pursuit of the Chiricahua Apaches in Arizona, 1883.

BILLY DIXON & ADOBE WALLS by *Billy Dixon and Edward Campbell Little*—Scout, Plainsman & Buffalo Hunter, *Life and Adventures of "Billy" Dixon* by Billy Dixon and *The Battle of Adobe Walls* by Edward Campbell Little (*Pearson's Magazine*).

WITH THE CALIFORNIA COLUMN by *George H. Petis*—Against Confederates and Hostile Indians During the American Civil War on the South Western Frontier, *The California Column, Frontier Service During the Rebellion* and *Kit Carson's Fight With the Comanche and Kiowa Indians*.

THRILLING DAYS IN ARMY LIFE by *George Alexander Forsyth*—Experiences of the Beecher's Island Battle 1868, the Apache Campaign of 1882, and the American Civil War.

INDIAN FIGHTS AND FIGHTERS by *Cyrus Townsend Brady*—Indian Fights and Fighters of the American Western Frontier of the 19th Century.

THE NEZ PERCÉ CAMPAIGN, 1877 by *G. O. Shields & Edmond Stephen Meany*—Two Accounts of Chief Joseph and the Defeat of the Nez Percé, *The Battle of Big Hole* by G. O. Shields and *Chief Joseph, the Nez Percé* by Edmond Stephen Meany.

CAPTAIN JEFF OF THE TEXAS RANGERS by *W. J. Maltby*—Fighting Comanche & Kiowa Indians on the South Western Frontier 1863-1874.

SHERIDAN'S TROOPERS ON THE BORDERS by *De Benneville Randolph Keim*—The Winter Campaign of the U. S. Army Against the Indian Tribes of the Southern Plains, 1868-9.

WILD LIFE IN THE FAR WEST by *James Hobbs*—The Adventures of a Hunter, Trapper, Guide, Prospector and Soldier.

THE OLD SANTA FE TRAIL by *Henry Inman*—The Story of a Great Highway.

LIFE IN THE FAR WEST by *George F. Ruxton*—The Experiences of a British Officer in America and Mexico During the 1840's.

ADVENTURES IN MEXICO AND THE ROCKY MOUNTAINS by *George F. Ruxton*—Experiences of Mexico and the South West During the 1840's.

LEONAUR

ALSO FROM LEONAUR
AVAILABLE IN SOFTCOVER OR HARDCOVER WITH DUST JACKET

FARAWAY CAMPAIGN *by F. James*—Experiences of an Indian Army Cavalry Officer in Persia & Russia During the Great War.

REVOLT IN THE DESERT *by T. E. Lawrence*—An account of the experiences of one remarkable British officer's war from his own perspective.

MACHINE-GUN SQUADRON *by A. M. G.*—The 20th Machine Gunners from British Yeomanry Regiments in the Middle East Campaign of the First World War.

A GUNNER'S CRUSADE *by Antony Bluett*—The Campaign in the Desert, Palestine & Syria as Experienced by the Honourable Artillery Company During the Great War .

DESPATCH RIDER *by W. H. L. Watson*—The Experiences of a British Army Motorcycle Despatch Rider During the Opening Battles of the Great War in Europe.

TIGERS ALONG THE TIGRIS *by E. J. Thompson*—The Leicestershire Regiment in Mesopotamia During the First World War.

HEARTS & DRAGONS *by Charles R. M. F. Crutwell*—The 4th Royal Berkshire Regiment in France and Italy During the Great War, 1914-1918.

INFANTRY BRIGADE: 1914 *by John Ward*—The Diary of a Commander of the 15th Infantry Brigade, 5th Division, British Army, During the Retreat from Mons.

DOING OUR 'BIT' *by Ian Hay*—Two Classic Accounts of the Men of Kitchener's 'New Army' During the Great War including *The First 100,000 & All In It*.

AN EYE IN THE STORM *by Arthur Ruhl*—An American War Correspondent's Experiences of the First World War from the Western Front to Gallipoli-and Beyond.

STAND & FALL *by Joe Cassells*—With the Middlesex Regiment Against the Bolsheviks 1918-19.

RIFLEMAN MACGILL'S WAR *by Patrick MacGill*—A Soldier of the London Irish During the Great War in Europe including *The Amateur Army, The Red Horizon & The Great Push*.

ON THE BORDER WITH CROOK *by John G. Bourke*—Personal Recollections of the American Indian Wars by an Officer on General Crook's Staff.

THE BUSH WAR DOCTOR *by Robert V. Dolbey*—The Experiences of a British Army Doctor During the East African Campaign of the First World War.

www.ingramcontent.com/pod-product-compliance
Lightning Source LLC
Chambersburg PA
CBHW020504100426
42813CB00030B/3106/J